The Nonviolent Life

Also by John Dear:

Disarming the Heart

Jean Donovan and the Call to Discipleship

Christ Is With the Poor: Writings of Horace McKenna

It's a Sin to Build a Nuclear Weapon: Writings of Richard McSorley

Our God Is Nonviolent

Oscar Romero and the Nonviolent Struggle for Justice

Seeds of Nonviolence

The God of Peace: Toward a Theology of Nonviolence

The Sacrament of Civil Disobedience

Peace Behind Bars

Apostle of Peace: Essays in Honor of Daniel Berrigan

Jesus the Rebel

The Road to Peace: Writings of Henri Nouwen

The Sound of Listening

The Vision of Peace: Writings of Mairead Maguire

And the Risen Bread: Selected Poems of Daniel Berrigan

Living Peace

Mohandas Gandhi: Essential Writings

Mary of Nazareth, Prophet of Peace

The Questions of Jesus

Transfiguration

You Will Be My Witnesses

The Advent of Peace

A Persistent Peace: An Autobiography

Put Down Your Sword

Daniel Berrigan: Essential Writings

Lazarus, Come Forth!

The Nonviolent Life

John Dear

Pace e Bene Press

The Nonviolent Life by John Dear
Published by Pace e Bene Press,
P.O. Box 1891, Long Beach, CA 90801
To order individual copies or bulk copies,
visit: www.paceebene.org or call 510-268-8765.

Author's Website: www.johndear.org

Library of Congress Cataloging-in-Publication Data
Dear, John 1959-
The Nonviolent Life / John Dear
ISBN-13: 978-0-9669783-2-2
ISBN-10: 0966978323

Library of Congress Control Number: 2013915471

Cover artwork by Carmelita Laura Valdes Damron.
Cover artwork copyright © 2013 Carmelita Laura Valdes Damron.
Design and layout: Ryan Hall

For Dar Williams and Patty Smythe,

Friends and Peacemakers

We are constantly being astonished these days at the amazing discoveries in the field of violence. But I maintain that far more undreamt of and seemingly impossible discoveries will be made in the field of nonviolence.

— Mohandas Gandhi

To me, nonviolence is the all-important virtue to be nourished and studied and cultivated.

— Dorothy Day

The ultimate weakness of violence is that it is a descending spiral begetting the very thing it seeks to destroy. Instead of diminishing evil, it multiplies it. Through violence you may murder the liar, but you cannot murder the lie, nor establish the truth. Through violence you murder the hater, but you do not murder hate. In fact, violence merely increases hate. Returning violence for violence multiplies violence, adding deeper darkness to a night already devoid of stars. Darkness cannot drive out darkness; only light can do that. Hate cannot drive out hate; only love can do that.

— Martin Luther King, Jr.

Contents

Foreword

We are living in an age when the immense power and potential of nonviolence is steadily being revealed.

Long dismissed as utopian, naïve, simplistic, impractical—and even unpatriotic and counter-productive—nonviolence is increasingly being activated in small ways and large to make powerful and effective change. And not a moment too soon.

The catastrophic challenges we face today—climate change, global poverty, permanent war, systematic violations of human rights, and many others—will not be solved by more violence. Effective solutions to these cataclysmic dangers will require monumental problem solving that is innovative, courageous, intentional, comprehensively universal, and compassionate. In short, the power of active and creative nonviolence is needed now more than ever.

Fortunately we are living in an era when this nonviolent power is being progressively unleashed around the world. And we are doubly fortunate because, not only is nonviolence increasingly being embodied and activated, it is also being understood and communicated in new and powerful ways.

A growing community of writers, artists, film-makers, theologians, educators and advocates for change are telling the stories of nonviolence, interpreting nonviolence, teaching nonviolence, and illuminating the dynamics of nonviolence.

Some—like the handful of friends who created the website *Waging Nonviolence*—are daily serving up case studies of ordinary people everywhere putting nonviolence into practice. Others—like Sharon Ellison, who created *Taking the War Out of Our Words: The Art of Powerful Non-Defensive Communication*—are crafting concrete tools that we can use in our everyday life. And some—like activist George Lakey who has spent a lifetime focused on nonviolence training and movement-building, or pioneering nonviolence scholar Gene Sharp—are illuminating in clear and convincing ways how nonviolent people-power works.

And then there are those who connect the dots—who draw these many facets of nonviolence together in a comprehensive framework for transforming our lives and our world.

John Dear is one of these.

In this book, Dear articulates a vision of the power, meaning and impact of the spiritually grounded nonviolent life—and invites us to put this into practice in both immediate and long-term ways.

Rooted in his journey as a follower of the nonviolent Jesus, Dear sets out in the following pages to unpack the three fundamental dimensions of the nonviolent journey: practicing nonviolence toward ourselves; practicing nonviolence toward all others; and practicing nonviolence by joining the global movement to abolish war, end poverty, stop the destruction of the earth, and to foster the well-being of all.

Dear not only illuminates each of these aspects of the nonviolent life, he shows that they are irreducibly interrelated. The nonviolent path is personal, interpersonal and global, and each dimension depends on the others.

For over three decades, Dear has been consciously experimenting with the power of nonviolence in his own life and in innumerable movements for change. He has written nearly thirty books on nonviolence, and has traveled the world sharing what he has learned flowing from his active meditation on the centrality of Jesus' inconveniently provocative message: *love your enemies, turn the other cheek, put down the sword.* These learnings have been distilled in this book.

This volume reflects the urgency of the great choice we face as a species: will we choose to continue to affirm a culture of systemic violence—or will we build a culture of active, creative and liberating nonviolence so that we can not only survive but thrive?

This urgency, infusing every page of this book, comes through in its narrative style. Dear makes bold statements about violence and about the nonviolent future. He does not mince words. He wants to capture our attention and bypass the carefully constructed filters that numb us to ubiquitous violence. Most of all, he wants to help us glimpse the breathtaking possibilities of the nonviolent option, and a life lived making that option a reality in our existence and in our world.

The novelist Flannery O'Connor, when asked why she created grotesque characters, indicated that she made them as large and vivid as she did so the reader would actually *see* them. Similarly, Dear makes blunt and bold declarations throughout this book to help us *see* the predicament we are in—and to *see* the powerful alternatives we have at our disposal.

This is why you will find the word "nonviolence" on virtually every page. This book is a straightforward, full on, incessant appeal to all of us to explore and try out this power—in our relationships, our communities, and our societies. This ubiquity of the word "nonviolence" is reminiscent of what St. Bonaventure wrote about St. Francis of Assisi in his book *The Journey of the Mind to God*: "At the beginning and end of every sermon Francis announced peace; in every greeting he wished for peace; in every contemplation he sighed for ecstatic peace." For Dear, it is nonviolence—the active embodiment of the peace Francis declared and lived, rooted in the infinite peace of God—that suffuses his work and his writing, including this book.

This volume presupposes the powerful theological revolution of the past half-century that has illuminated the nonviolence of Jesus. A wide range of scripture scholars and theologians—including Howard Thurman, André Trocmé, Bernard Haring, John Howard Yoder, Thomas Merton, James W. Douglass, Daniel Berrigan, Ched Myers, Richard Horsley, Walter Wink, John Dominic Crossan and others—have carefully and patiently revealed Jesus' vision and practice of nonviolence. Dear sees his task here less of re-presenting these findings (readers are invited to read this growing literature on the nonviolent Jesus) than in exploring what their implications are for us today and how they can guide our way forward.

This is a clarion call, underscored by a declaration that recurs throughout the book: "the days of violence are over." The old ways, patterns, theologies, and myths of redemptive violence are finished. Each time he declares this in the book we are jarred, caught off guard. It is a baffling declaration, but it is so blatant and clear that it can snap us to attention: we are being asked to affirm this, to take it seriously and then—most challengingly—to do something about it. Can we end violence? In our lives? In our relationships? In our world? Dear's phrasing is both daunting and deeply hopeful—because if the days of violence are over, that means the days of definitive nonviolence are finally beginning.

But, as Dear also suggests, we can miss this opportunity. Sprinkled throughout this book is the phrase: "Life is short." It implies that we don't have time to dither. There's not a moment to waste. Our chance *can* pass us by. We are therefore called to respond to the critical call at this moment in history to move the nonviolent revolution forward, using whatever time we have left.

Dear has written this volume to be read, to be pondered, and to provoke both discussion and action. There is a set of questions after each of the three parts of the book, which study groups, prayer groups, book clubs and whole movements can mull on together.

In this book you are invited to explore John Dear's urgent diagnosis of the calamity that's bearing down on us, but also his dramatic and soulful prescription for healing our lives and our planet. Together, we can experiment with, embody, and deeply live the nonviolent life.

Ken Butigan

Prayer for a Nonviolent Life

God of peace, thank you for being gentle, loving, compassionate, and nonviolent! You are so nonviolent that you do not force yourself upon us, but gently call us to your wisdom and way of nonviolence. You give us the freedom to do as we will. Help us to do your will of peace, to choose your way of nonviolence. Help us to live nonviolent lives, to become your holy people of nonviolence, to welcome your reign of peace and nonviolence here on earth.

Help me to be nonviolent to myself. Give me the grace to let go of violence, to love and accept myself, to treat myself nonviolently, to cultivate inner peace, and to dwell in your peace. Send your Holy Spirit of peace upon me that I might live in relationship with you as your beloved child, that I might know your love and healing peace, love you in return and honor you by taking care of myself and being nonviolent to myself for the rest of my life.

Help me to practice loving nonviolence toward everyone I know and meet, that I might love my neighbor as myself, and never hurt anyone ever again. Help me to be nonviolent to all creatures and all creation, that I may spread your peace far and wide to all sentient beings, to your beautiful creation. Give me a heart as wide as the world that I might love everyone around the world, even those targeted as "enemies" by my nation. Open my heart to love every human being as my sister and brother, that I might practice your universal nonviolent love from now on.

Help me to serve your reign of peace by joining the global grassroots movement of nonviolence. Make me an instrument of your peace, that I might do my part to help abolish war, poverty, hunger, racism, sexism, executions, nuclear weapons, systemic injustice and environmental destruction, and welcome your nonviolent reign of peace with justice here on earth. Bless this grassroots movement of nonviolence with your wisdom, your determination, and your persistent action that we might see "justice roll down like waters" and welcome new breakthroughs of justice and peace every day.

As I follow the nonviolent Jesus on the path of peace and love, help me to claim my true identity as your beloved son/daughter, that I might always live in your peace and love, and serve your reign of peace and love, now and forever.

Thank you. Amen.

Introduction

It was a typical week in our world of violence. Dozens killed in explosions in Iraq; U.S. drone attacks in Afghanistan; the ongoing U.S.-backed occupation of Palestine; the forced-feeding of U.S. prisoners at Guantanamo; the U.S. president's perusal of his assassination list; millions of children starving to death around the world; ongoing preparations for nuclear war; the continued exploitation of the earth and its creatures; over one thousand killed in the collapse of a corrupt Bangladeshi garment worker factory; inner city shootings; fifteen dead from a fiery factory explosion in Texas—and the Boston marathon bombings.

On Monday April 15, 2013, two young brothers set off massive homemade bombs at the finish line of the Boston marathon, killing three and injuring some 260 others. The nation reeled in shock, as it had a few months earlier on December 14, 2012, when twenty school children and six adults were killed at the Sandy Hook Elementary School in Connecticut, and before that, on July 20, 2012, when twelve moviegoers were killed and seventy injured in Aurora, Colorado, and before that on April 16, 2007, when thirty-two people were killed and seventeen wounded at Virginia Tech.

Throughout the intensive media coverage of the Boston Marathon bombings, people grieved and expressed outrage. All the while, the U.S. continued to kill thousands of people in Afghanistan, Iraq, Libya, Pakistan, Yemen and elsewhere.

One of those killed at the Boston marathon finish line was eight-year-old Martin Richard from Dorchester, Massachusetts. He came with his family to watch his father cross the line. Martin was blown up instantly, and his mother and sister were seriously wounded.

The next day, friends released a photo of Martin standing in his school classroom, smiling and holding a handmade poster with

1

two red hearts and a peace sign. His poster read: "No More Hurting People. Peace." He made the poster at school in response to the shooting of young Trayvon Martin in Florida not long before. He wanted the violence to stop.

No More Hurting People! Peace!

When I saw that photo I thought to myself: this is the voice of God speaking to us all. It is the cry of the world's children. It is the message of Jesus and Buddha, Francis and Gandhi, Dorothy Day and Rosa Parks, passed on to us down through the ages.

This cry for peace should be our headline, our mantra, our communal wisdom, our theme song, our one topic, our goal, our public policy, our new bottom line. It should be the basis for a new foreign policy, for religion, for all politics from now on.

Young Martin's photo should have been on the cover of *Time* and *The New York Times*, but I'm sure it was dismissed by the mainstream media because, ultimately, it was too serious and too powerful. It ran against the grain of our government and its military, its wars and violent policies which hurt so many. As far as the media is concerned, violence sells. Peace does not. We can't stir people up with a photo of a dead child calling for peace. They might actually take it to heart and do something!

I think Martin Richard was smarter than all the pundits, politicians, warmakers and their chaplains put together. His wisdom and message stand at the heart of truth and reality. "Hurting one another doesn't work," I hear him saying. "You reap what you sow. Violence in response to violence only leads to further violence. All violence is terrorism. War never leads to peace. Those who live by the sword will die by the sword. Preparing to use nuclear bombs is the ultimate form of terrorism. We should stop our terrorist warmaking. We need to stop the killing, stop the bombing, stop the starving, stop all the unjust dying. The days of hurting others are over. Let's all live in peace."

The Violent Life

It would be comical, if it weren't so tragic, when our politicians and pundits ask, "Why would anyone do such a thing to us?" We as a people are blind and naïve to the terrorism we Americans do to the world's children, not to mention the terrorism we prepare to do with our drones and nuclear weapons. These deadly preparations do not go unnoticed. We are inspiring millions of people to hate us. It's virtually inevitable that a few of them will go insane with hatred and suicidal terrorism, and attack us.

During my 2012 visit to Afghanistan, I heard many stories about how our drones and fighter bombers blew up loved ones. In the face of these American bombing raids, anyone of us would likely be tempted to join the Taliban. The question is not, "Why would anyone do such a thing to us?" but rather, "Why doesn't everyone in the world hate us and want to kill us?" This is the legacy of decades of warmaking, bombings, terrorist attacks and nuclear threats.

For decades, the U.S. has been bombing and killing children around the world—from Vietnam and Nicaragua, to El Salvador and Colombia, to Iraq and Afghanistan, Yemen and Pakistan. This global spree of violence which we spread around the world will inevitably whiplash back upon us. That's the way violence works. It's a never-ending downward spiral that brings death to everyone. It always comes back upon those who first wield it. In his book *Blowback*, scholar Chalmers Johnson carefully documented how the violence perpetrated by the U.S. government provokes violent retaliation. Yet we continue to spend trillions on warmaking, build nuclear weapons, and act as if killing people was normal and reasonable. Much of our society, including the churches, remains silent about this growing culture of permanent war.

If we do not want any more bombings here at home, we must stop bombing people abroad and figure out a way to live in peace with everyone on the planet.

If we justify our all-American violence and warmaking, why shouldn't millions of our victims feel justified to do violence against us? So goes the age-old policy—"an eye for an eye, and a tooth for a tooth"—which Gandhi said just leaves us all blind and toothless, armless and legless, and maybe just plain dead.

That's the way of the world, and the predicament that we all find ourselves in these days. A world of total violence—with 30 wars, a billion people starving, 3 billion people living in poverty, 20,000 nuclear weapons on alert, corporate greed decimating the world's poor, and catastrophic climate change threatening us all. This world of permanent war, greed and destruction has become normal, routine, and legal. We have grown used to it. Violence is everywhere, and we typically come to the conclusion that there's nothing that can be done about it.

We think of guns, drones, bombs and nuclear weapons as "necessary" evils. We don't even speak of progress toward a more peaceful world. It's violence morning, noon and night. It surrounds us, overwhelms us, eats away at us, and consumes us. Indeed, it has become a plague that touches everyone, a virus that infects and spreads and kills.

If we want to speak of a new "nonviolent life" for ourselves, we have to recognize first of all the current life we lead—our "violent life."

We are violent. And our violence has made us selfish, narcissistic, fearful, unwise and miserable. We hurt one another, kill one another, ignore the deaths of millions, and do nothing to stop the spread of this plague of violence. Violence is, for us, a way of life. Or rather, a way of death that masquerades as a way of life.

The time has come to end violence as a way of life because it only brings death. It does not work, it does not make us happy, it

4

does not lead to any kind of progress except further violence and death.

The time has come to unlearn the ways of violence and to learn the way of nonviolence. Just as the alcoholic can choose to give up the bottle and become sober, people of violence can renounce violence and become sober people of nonviolence. This is possible. As we move closer to the brink of global destruction, it is, in fact, the only sane, rational, intelligent choice to make.

In this book, I propose that each one of us: reject violence as a way of life and consciously choose to live a life of nonviolence; practice and teach others the way of nonviolence; and do our part to build a global grassroots movement of nonviolence. This is our only alternative in the face of our committed violence, global illness, and common insanity. We need to work toward committed nonviolence, global healing and common sanity.

Turning From Violence to Nonviolence

In the months after the Boston marathon bombings, I sat with Martin Richard's sign. It helped me grieve and gave me hope. His sign points us in the right direction of nonviolence toward a new world of peace. Nonviolence, he suggests, is the only remedy for the insanity of global terrorism, endless war, and the epidemic of violence that we have unleashed upon ourselves.

Martin gave voice to the great demand that life itself places before us all. How can we help stop inflicting violence and death on ourselves, other people, all creatures and creation itself?

First of all, we have to examine our own lives and ask ourselves: how do we cultivate violence within ourselves? How do we hurt ourselves, how are we violent to ourselves, how do we nurse violence within us, how do we personally support the sickness of violence in our own personal lives—and what do we need to do to stop cooperating with our own violence and start cultivating interior and personal nonviolence?

5

Next, we need to ask: who are the people we have hurt in the past, and who are we hurting now? How can we stop hurting them? If we find that we are hurting one person, let us take immediate action to stop hurting them, apologize to them and help them heal. And then, we can start asking ourselves: how can we be nonviolent toward every human being from now on?

Then, we need to explore the communities and places where we belong and ask in a similar vein: Whom are we collectively hurting, and how can we stop hurting them? At school, in our religious communities, at the workplace, in our cities—how do we personally support the collective violence inflicted by some upon others, and what can we do to stop that violence?

Finally, we can ask: who are the people we as a nation are hurting, and how can we stop our nation from hurting others? For Americans, that list is long. If we were to take this child of peace seriously, we would have to withdraw all troops from Afghanistan immediately; make restitution to the people of Afghanistan and Iraq; stop our drone program; close Guantanamo; enact tough anti-gun legislation; end the death penalty; dismantle our nuclear weapons, Trident submarines and fighter bombers; feed the world's starving poor; educate the world in peacemaking; and fund nonviolent conflict resolution programs around the world so that people everywhere can tap the transformative power of active nonviolence and welcome a more just, peaceful world.

This vision of nonviolence is not a pipe dream. It is the message of all spiritual traditions and all peacemakers. It's the message of Mahatma Gandhi, Dr. Martin Luther King, Jr., Dorothy Day, Rabbi Abraham Heschel, Abdul Gaffar Kahn, Adolfo Perez Esquivel, Mairead Maguire, Archbishop Oscar Romero, Muriel Lester, Pope John XXIII, Leymah Gbowee, Aung San Sui Kyi, Daniel Berrigan, Rosa Parks, Rigoberta Menchu, Mother Teresa, Archbishop Desmond Tutu, Thich Nhat Hanh and the Dalai Lama. It's certainly the message of the nonviolent Jesus who calls us to "love our enemies." Martin

Richard simply joined his hopes to the aspirations of our greatest peacemakers.

These champions of peace held that the rights of children trump all national, corporate and militaristic interests, especially the right of every child not to be victimized by the violence of poverty and war. This kind of foreign policy demands that no child will ever be hurt again. There is no cause worth the death of a single child. Since the risk of hurting one child is too great, from now on, we must pursue the abolition of poverty, hunger, war, nuclear weapons, environmental destruction and violence of all kinds.

War and weapons have failed to bring about a world of peace. Creative nonviolence, on the other hand, works whenever it is tried. That's what the historical record now proves. If we spend trillions of dollars, not on war and weapons, but on the means of peace—such as nonviolent civilian based defense systems, nonviolent international peace teams, nonviolent intervention, diplomacy, dialogue, and nonviolent responses to terrorism—people can live in peace. If we stop our own terrorist attacks—such as our drone raids on impoverished villages—and fund global food and clean water distribution, free universal healthcare, low income housing and schools, we could not only win the world over and end terrorism, we could abolish war and poverty. We would make our world safer for children, and start us down a new path toward universal love and economic justice.

"Humanity must put an end to war or war will put an end to humanity," Dr. King preached at the National Cathedral a few days before the U.S. government killed him. "It is no longer a choice, my friends, between violence and nonviolence," he said. "It is either nonviolence or nonexistence, and the alternative to disarmament, the alternative to a greater suspension of nuclear tests, the alternative to strengthening the United Nations and thereby disarming the whole world, may well be an inferno that even the mind of Dante could not imagine."

"Humanity has to get out of violence only by nonviolence," Gandhi wrote. "Hatred can be overcome only by love. Counter-hatred only increases the surface as well as the depth of hatred. We have to make truth and nonviolence not matters for mere individual practice but for practice by groups and communities and nations. That at any rate is my dream."

For the sake of Martin Richard, Martin King, Mahatma Gandhi, and all victims of violence, we need to pursue the dream of nonviolence and agree not to hurt others but instead to work for an end to policies, structures, institutions and systems which hurt people everywhere. That means that each one of us has to renounce our violent behavior, become a person of creative nonviolence, and get involved as activists, organizers, and foot soldiers in the global grassroots movement of nonviolence so that one day the world's children might live in peace.

The Three Dimensions of the Nonviolent Life

How can we become people of nonviolence and help the world become more nonviolent? What does it mean to be a person of active nonviolence? How can we help build a global grassroots movement of nonviolence to disarm the world, relieve unjust human suffering, make a more just society and protect creation and all creatures? What is a nonviolent life?

In this little book, I propose a simple vision of nonviolence that every one of us can aspire to. I commend three dimensions of nonviolence—practicing nonviolence toward ourselves; practicing nonviolence toward all others, all creatures and creation; and practicing active nonviolence by joining the global grassroots movement of nonviolence—and suggest that to be a person of nonviolence, we each need to practice each dimension simultaneously if we are to become authentic practitioners of nonviolence.

Many of us do practice one, or maybe two, of these dimensions. We might be nonviolent toward ourselves and most others, but we are not part of the global movement of nonviolence. Or we might be committed activists involved in the movements for justice and peace, but filled with self hatred or mean toward those around us.

The nonviolent life in all its fullness demands that we practice all three dimensions at the same time! It's like straddling a tightrope, or juggling three bowling pins, or for that matter, walking on water. We are called to a new kind of centered mindfulness where we consciously practice an interior and exterior nonviolence, where we practice nonviolence in our private lives as well as work publicly and actively in the movements for disarmament, justice and peace through creative nonviolence. It means becoming in our own ordinariness new Gandhis, Kings, and Dorothy Days.

That's the invitation of the nonviolent life—to be nonviolent to ourselves, to be nonviolent to all others, and to be part of the global movement of nonviolence that is slowly sweeping across the world. Such a comprehensive vision is not about perfection; indeed, we never become perfectly nonviolent. Nor can nonviolence be achieved overnight. It is, instead, an ongoing journey toward the fullness of life, where every step can be peaceful, and every outcome can be healing and transformative.

Living a Nonviolent Life

To integrate these three dimensions of nonviolence seamlessly into our lives takes steadfast commitment, mindful attention and calm patience. We need to train ourselves in the methodologies and practice of nonviolence to unleash the holy, holistic power of nonviolence in every part of our individual, interpersonal and global lives. As we do, we will discover, as Dr. King did, a peaceful way to live and deal with the world. "I plan to stand by nonviolence," he said shortly before he died, "because I have found it to be a philosophy of life that regulates not only my dealings in the struggle for racial justice but also my dealings with people and with my own self."

As we take new steps forward in the nonviolent life, we will discover, to our amazement, how to be more peaceful and what it means to be a human being.

I believe we were created to be nonviolent, that the whole human family was designed by the God of peace to live and practice nonviolence. Organized religion, schools and universities, and the world's governments should therefore teach, practice and pass on the wisdom of nonviolence. Because we have given ourselves over to the forces and systems of violence instead, we have to teach ourselves how to be nonviolent, and get involved personally in creating grassroots movements of nonviolence, if the world is to survive.

More than that, nonviolence is what the spiritual life is all about. God, we are learning, is a God of nonviolence. A Godly life, then, is a nonviolent life. Every one of us is on a journey toward our loving, nonviolent God. Along the way, we discover the God of nonviolence within us and among us. In this lifelong pilgrimage, we come to rely on the living God of nonviolence and peace, and to renounce the false gods of violence and war. The God of peace becomes the focus of our lives, and we seek to serve the God of peace as instruments of God's peace.

This is our great quest.

This is the purpose and meaning of life.

With this book, I invite you to examine your own life within the framework of nonviolence. When did you begin to move out of the culture of violence and war into the new life of nonviolence and peace? Where are you on the road to peace, as we turn around from the path of violence and war onto the way of peace and nonviolence? How are you violent and how can you become more and more nonviolent? What can we do to help others become more nonviolent? How do we work for a new world of nonviolence? How does nonviolence affect our understanding of the spiritual life, theology, organized religion, education, economics, politics, self-defense, national defense, global defense, and our very humanity? How can we become peacemakers who create peace around us? What can we do with the time we have left on earth to help abolish war, poverty, starvation, handguns, nuclear weapons, environmental destruction, and the systems and structures of violence?

In other words, how can we become loving people of active nonviolence who spend every day from now on sowing the seeds of nonviolence that might one day lead to a new harvest of peace for humanity? How can we serve the God of peace and become authentic instruments of God's peace?

These are great questions. They demand that we wake up, turn off the TV, get our act together, recenter ourselves in the Holy Spirit of peace, and join the global movement of nonviolence for a new world of peace. Nothing is more important.

This book is intended to be read straight through. I propose that the life of nonviolence requires three simultaneous dimensions—nonviolence toward one's self, nonviolence towards all others, and participating in the global grassroots movement of nonviolence—and so I've broken the book into three sections to explore each one of those dimensions. So it will make most sense after all three dimensions of the nonviolent life are considered. If you read only part one, for instance, you will miss the point of the book. All three sections need to be held together and considered so that we can gain new insights into the fullness of the life of nonviolence.

In effect, the book—in its three sections—is simply an extrapolation of the opening "prayer for a nonviolent life." That prayer is the message of this book.

I invite you to use this book slowly for prayer and meditation, to help yourself deepen your own personal journey of nonviolence and your own involvement in the public work of peace and justice. Then, I invite you to order bulk copies of the book, and give it away to teachers, ministers, priests, politicians, relatives, children, activists, friends, neighbors and enemies, that others may start living the nonviolent life as well, that together we might spread the way and wisdom of nonviolence far and wide, in the hope that a new world of nonviolence may one day become a reality.

May the God of peace bless us with the wisdom and practice of nonviolence that we might become people of loving, active nonviolence who welcome God's nonviolent reign of peace on earth.

John Dear
July 4, 2013
Santa Fe, New Mexico

Part One

Nonviolence Toward Ourselves

Nonviolence is the greatest and most active force in the world. One person who can express nonviolence in life exercises a force superior to all the forces of brutality. My optimism rests on my belief in the infinite possibilities of the individual to develop nonviolence. The more you develop it in your own being, the more infectious it becomes till it overwhelms your surroundings and by and by might oversweep the world.

— Gandhi

Your nonviolence must shine through your speech, your action, your general behavior. A votary of nonviolence must cultivate a habit of unremitting toil, sleepless vigilance, and ceaseless self-control.

— Gandhi

Nonviolence is not like a garment to be put on and off at will. Its seat is in the heart and it must be an inseparable part of our very being.

— Gandhi

Devotion to nonviolence is the highest expression of humanity's conscious state.

— Gandhi

I think nonviolence is a very natural way of doing things, and violence is highly out of the ordinary.

— Cesar Chavez

1

Remembering Who We Already Are

Being a person of nonviolence means first of all being nonviolent to ourselves. But these days, through the culture's constant barrage of violence and war, we often hurt ourselves without even knowing it. So the journey of nonviolence begins by looking within, examining the violence inside us and its causes, and choosing to be more nonviolent to ourselves, so that then we will know how to be more nonviolent to others.

But what does it mean to be nonviolent? Coming from the Hindu/Sanskrit word *ahimsa*, nonviolence was defined long ago as "causing no harm, no injury, no violence to any living creature." But Mohandas Gandhi insisted that it means much more than that. He said nonviolence was the active, unconditional love towards others, the persistent pursuit of truth, the radical forgiveness toward those who hurt us, the steadfast resistance to every form of evil, and even the loving willingness to accept suffering in the struggle for justice without the desire for retaliation. All these themes describe both an entirely new way of life, as well as a new methodology for human living and social change.

Another way to understand nonviolence is to set it within the context of our identity. Practicing nonviolence means claiming our fundamental identity as the beloved sons and daughters of the God of peace, and thus, going forth into the world of war as peacemakers to love every other human being. We do that because we know who we are and we act as if we are truly God's beloved sons and daughters. This is what Jesus taught: "Blessed are the peacemakers; they shall be called the sons and daughters of God.... Love your enemies and pray for your persecutors, then you shall be sons and daughters of the God who makes his sun rise on the good and the bad, and causes rain to fall on the just and the unjust." In the context of his visionary nonviolence—radical peacemaking and love for enemies—Jesus speaks of being who we already are, the sons and daughters of God. He talks about our true identities as if they propel us to be people of loving nonviolence.

The problem is: we don't know who we are. We do not realize the depth of our true identities as sons and daughters of the God of peace and love. If we did know this at the very core of our being, we would all be nonviolent. But we forget who we are, or choose to ignore who we are, or actively deny who we are—and so we are violent to ourselves and others. The challenge then is to remember who we are, and therefore be nonviolent to ourselves and others.

Violence can be defined according to Charles McCarthy as forgetting who we are. It involves the rejection or forgetting of our ultimate identity—who we are in relation to the God of peace. Once we reject who we are, forget who we are, or fail to recognize who we are, we easily do violence to ourselves and others because we have lost ourselves in the chaos of meaninglessness. Just as we no longer realize our own identities, we forget that every other human being is our sister and brother. So we hurt ourselves and others, and even kill ourselves and others. This radical misunderstanding about what it means to be a human being is at the heart of our global chaos of violence.

Violence means forgetting our basic humanity, ignoring or not claiming our true identity as a human being, as a son or daughter of the God of peace, a brother or sister of every other human being. If we don't know we are God's beloved, if we forget that other people are our beloved sisters and brothers, we will end up killing people, building nuclear weapons, bombing people with our drones, or vaporizing people as we did in Hiroshima. This violence comes as a direct result of our "mindlessness." We go through life as sleep-walkers, unconscious, unaware and mindless, and become a danger to ourselves and others. We don't mind being violent to ourselves, or care about the unjust suffering and death of others. We don't care because we don't understand that we are all one, all children of our beloved God of peace, all sisters and brothers of one another.

Nonviolence can be defined as remembering who we are and recalling every day who we are, and constantly reclaiming the truth of reality—that we are all one, all of us sons and daughters of the God of peace, sisters and brothers of one another. Active nonviolence naturally flows from those who live fully within their fundamental identity as God's children through daily mindfulness and conscious awareness and who struggle to remain faithful to that core identity every moment for the rest of our lives.

Living nonviolence requires daily meditation, contemplation, study, concentration and mindfulness. Just as mindlessness leads to violence, steady mindfulness and conscious awareness of our true identities lead to nonviolence and peace. The deeper we go into mindful nonviolence, the more we live the truth of our identity as sisters and brothers of one another, and sons and daughters of the God of peace. The social, economic and political implications of this practice are astounding: if we are sons and daughters of a loving Creator, then every human being is our sister and brother, and we can never hurt anyone on earth ever again, much less be silent in the face of war, starvation, racism, sexism, nuclear weapons, systemic injustice and environmental destruction.

Nonviolence demands an active universal love for the whole human race which vigorously pursues the truth of our common humanity. We actively, publicly engage in the struggle for justice and peace because we love every human being as our sister and brother. We know that every human being is our very sister and brother, and so we give our lives to help everyone live in peace with justice. We want no one to suffer, much less to die from war, starvation, nuclear weapons or executions. Through our active nonviolence we consciously reconcile with every human being as

17

well as resist every structure, system and act of violence, in order to welcome God's nonviolent reign of justice, love and peace.

There is nothing passive about this life of nonviolence. It is an active way of life; it requires positive activity every day for the good of ourselves, all others and all creation. This positive, active, universal love springs from the inner awareness of true identity, our relationship to the God of peace, and the belovedness we claim for ourselves and everyone.

The culture of war and violence, on the other hand, is always trying to tell us who we are, to name us. Too often, we let it tell us who we are. And so, we claim many false, or secondary identities. We let the culture identify us as American, conservative or liberal, right or left, Democrat or Republican, and so forth. Some of us base our entire lives on a false identity. We don't know who we truly are, so we let the culture of war name us, and we end up going through life hurting ourselves and others, leaving behind a trail of wreckage.

Remember the TV commercial about the U.S. Marines? To "be all you can be," it said, join the Marines. In other words, join us, kill for the American empire, and you will reach your true identity. This, to me, is a total lie, the exact opposite of the truth of who we are. To "be all we can truly be" means becoming people of nonviolence, love and peace.

The Gospel calls us to become our true selves, to be the beloved sons and daughters of the God of peace who we already are by fulfilling our vocation to be life-giving peacemakers. In contrast, the military mimics this call but orients it toward warmaking and death, not the life of peace. It uses the question of our identity to recruit us into the culture of violence and war. Many fall for that old trick. But we need not any more.

One way then to understand Christianity is to hear the nonviolent Jesus tell us who we truly are. *You are the beloved sons and daughters of the God of peace*, he declares, *not the sons and daughters of the empire or the culture of war and violence.* As Christians, we try to take him at his word, claim our core identity and remain faithful to it. As we do, we go forth in the culture of war, make peace, resist empire, live in God's love and welcome God's reign of peace. We try to help everyone else know that they too are beloved sons and daughters of God, that they can be nonviolent, that they are loved and lovable and can love everyone. This is the meaning of life, the fullness of life, and the work of a peacemaking life.

How did Jesus Practice Perfect Nonviolence?

Gandhi said Jesus practiced perfect nonviolence. If that's true, then how was Jesus able to be so perfectly nonviolent? How did he practice such noble peacemaking? How did embody creative nonviolence so well? The answer can be found at the beginning of his story, at his baptism.

Sitting by the Jordan River in a moment of prayer, Jesus hears a voice say, "You are my beloved son; with you I am well pleased." Unlike most of us, Jesus accepts this announcement of God's love for him. He claims his true identity as the beloved son of the God of peace. From then on, he knows who he is. He's faithful to this identity until the moment he dies. From the desert to the cross, he is faithful to who he is. He becomes who he is, and lives up to who he is, and so he acts publicly like God's beloved.

This moment by the Jordan River, I think, holds the key to any understanding of Jesus' peacemaking life and creative nonviolence. How did he know that God was nonviolent and loving? Because he experienced God's love and nonviolence as he sat by the Jordan River. Overwhelmed by a nonviolent, loving God, who affirmed him and named him as "My beloved Son," Jesus decided to trust this nonviolent, loving God for the rest of his life. He decided to take God at God's word about his identity. Because he claimed that statement as his true core identity, he found uncommon inner strength to go forth into the culture of violence with astonishing love and creative nonviolence, to practice the love and nonviolence he first experienced from God.

After Jesus accepts his identity as the beloved son of the God of peace, he goes into the desert to pray and fast for forty days, and he's immediately tempted to renounce that identity, which means that he's tempted to do mindless violence and live a false spirituality of violence and war. The temptations begin: "Oh yeah? If you are the son of God, then prove it. Do this, do that…Do violence to yourself, be effective, worship power, lose your soul… Be a violent messiah, like the Roman Emperor, and serve the culture of violence and war."

In the desert, Jesus refuses to reject his true identity, and decides to live every moment of his life in relationship to the God of peace as God's beloved son. In doing so, he receives the strength to reject every temptation to violence and practice militant nonviolence. He remains faithful to that identity and relationship every moment for the rest of his life. Throughout his peacemaking life, people challenge that identity, whether the demons whom he was expelling or the religious authorities whom he was correcting. Even as he dies on the cross, the passers-by taunt him saying, "If you are the son of God, prove it: come down from that cross!" But he remains faithful to the voice that says "You are my beloved."

Knowing who he is, rooted in his relationship with the God of peace, Jesus remains peaceful. He embodies nonviolence and goes forth into the world of war to make peace. Because he trusts so fully in his nonviolent, loving God, he goes to his death practicing perfect nonviolent love. He does not try to respond with violence, lose his faith, or rage with anger. Instead, he forgives his killers and surrenders himself in peace to the God of peace. His death becomes a spiritual explosion that continues to disarm millions across the centuries.

If he had renounced his identity, he would have done violence and become like any other warmaker. Because he remained faithful to the God of peace and God's love for him, he was centered in peace and able to practice astonishing nonviolent love, the kind that lays down one's life for others.

Claiming Our True Identities and Practicing Nonviolence

If the story ended there, that would be enough. But in his "Sermon on the Mount" teachings on peace and nonviolence, Jesus throws open the invitation to the whole human race! "Blessed are the peacemakers; they are the sons and daughters of the God of peace," he says. In other words, *everyone* can be a beloved son or daughter of the God of peace, *everyone* can become a nonviolent peacemaker, *everyone* is called "My Beloved" by the God of peace, *everyone* can claim their true identity as a son or daughter of the God of peace.

Jesus connects the question of our identity—who are really we—to peacemaking, nonviolence, and universal love. Love your enemies, he teaches at the high point of his sermon, then you are really sons and daughters of the God of universal nonviolent love, "the God who makes his sun to rise on the good and the bad, and causes rain to fall on the just and the unjust."

Most people throughout history have missed this point, I submit. Jesus treats every human being as his beloved brother or sister, as a beloved son or daughter of his beloved God. Therefore, he sees the potential of peacemaking and active nonviolence in every one of us, and calls everyone he meets to disarm and realize their holy potential, to become who they already are, to fulfill their true identity in God, just as he does, and so, to become peacemakers who practice universal, nonviolent love.

If Jesus' story is the fullest realization of everyone's story, then God says to every one of us at some point, "You are my beloved." Few, however, hear this proclamation, much less embrace it as true. If we could hear this invitation and claim this amazing truth, we too could become peacemaking people of nonviolence. We would spend our lives fulfilling this calling, seeing everyone as a sister and brother, and giving our lives like Jesus to help others realize their vocation in the God of peace.

This insight is, I believe, the key to Christian nonviolence, the spiritual life, and our very humanity. As we hear God's voice and understand who we are, we accept ourselves and one another as God's beloved sons and daughters. In that spirit, we renounce any violence toward ourselves or another, seek never to harm ourselves or any sister or brother again, try to be more nonviolent to ourselves and one another, and join God's global movement of nonviolence to disarm the world and welcome God's peace on earth.

I've never heard anyone explain the spiritual life in these terms before, except perhaps my friend Henri Nouwen who was beginning to explore this theme in the last few years of his life, particularly in his book, *Life of the Beloved*. This is the key to our work for peace with justice: we are the beloved sons and daughters of the God of peace, and so we go forth into the world of war to make peace. More, this is the true identity of everyone, though few know it or claim it. That's why nonviolence can be defined as remembering and recalling every day in our meditation who we are: the beloved sons and daughters of the God of peace, sisters and brothers of every human being on the planet, people of universal, nonviolent love. Because we trust the God of love and peace, we do not fear; we go forward in faith, hope and universal love to practice creative nonviolence in the world of violence. We try to be true to our identities, and so like Jesus, we give our lives for our suffering sisters and brothers, to welcome God's reign of peace with justice.

Over time, this realization of our true identity challenges and changes our understanding of God. We come to know God not as a god of violence, hatred or war, but as the living God of nonviolence, love and peace. It challenges and changes our understanding of what the church should be. Now we know that the church is supposed to be a community of peace, love and nonviolence, a place to help us all be who we already are and send us forth to make peace. It also transforms our understanding of what life is about. Instead of making money, getting by, or getting ahead, life becomes a journey of disarming our hearts and our world, and actively welcoming instead a new world of peace, God's reign of nonviolence right here in our midst.

The more we can claim our core identities as God's beloved sons and daughters, and therefore as the beloved brothers and sisters of one another, the better we will be able to practice nonviolence like Jesus, and fulfill the mission of peace that he sends us on. As we honor who we are, we will start to be more nonviolent to ourselves, and non-cooperate with our own inner violence, so that the God of peace, the One who tells us who we are, can dwell at peace within us.

2

Cultivating Interior Nonviolence

We are all called to become who we were created to be—the beloved sons and daughters of the God of peace. That means, that each one of us is sent like the nonviolent Jesus into the world of war to make peace. We claim our true identities in God's love, and try to love ourselves, every one we meet, and to increase love and end violence throughout the world. This is a beautiful, exciting mission which gives our lives ultimate meaning in the universal scheme of things.

Rooted in this identity and mission, we seek to live in the conscious awareness of God's loving presence, and to share that disarming love with everyone. That means, we continue to nurture God's peace and nonviolence within us, every day, for the rest of our lives. We strive to become people of peace, who act like the sons and daughters of the God of peace. We seek to let that holy peace dwell within us and radiate from us so that the world will become more peaceful, more nonviolent.

Of course, this is much harder than it sounds. That's why I suggest that we begin our reflections on the life of nonviolence with the inner work of nonviolence—letting go of our interior violence, cultivating interior nonviolence, not being violent to ourselves, and working to treat ourselves nonviolently from now on. We need to practice nonviolence first of all toward ourselves, and never again be violent to ourselves. The life of nonviolence begins as we befriend ourselves, make peace with ourselves, and make room for God's Spirit of peace to live and dwell within us. It means taking to heart God's affirming word of love and seeing ourselves through that lens of nonviolent love as God does.

Most of us find this difficult to do. We're used to violence, even violence toward ourselves. We don't like ourselves, punish ourselves, put ourselves down, even physically hurt ourselves. We actively cultivate and nurture our inner violence. Some of us can't even imagine being nonviolent toward ourselves. We don't love our neighbors as ourselves, as the Gospels instruct, because, first of all, most of us don't love ourselves.

We don't like to talk about it, but there's an epidemic of self-hatred, low self-esteem, inner violence and suicide across the land. If we're going to be nonviolent to others, we have to make sure first that we are nonviolent to ourselves. The life of nonviolence notices and rejects our inner violence, learns to cultivate inner nonviolence, and over time, helps us to be nonviolent toward ourselves and feel more peaceful within. From that inner space of peace and nonviolence, we will be able to offer peace and nonviolence to the world.

Inner Violence and Inner Nonviolence

Start by looking at the violence within. What's going on inside you? How do you feel about yourself, your life, your body, your spirit, your soul? Do you ever put yourself down? Do you have any areas or feelings of violence toward yourself? Because we have all been raised in a culture of violence, we all have moments of self-hatred and violence toward ourselves. We have all internalized violence to some degree. The key is to grow in awareness of that inner violence, let go of it, cultivate inner nonviolence instead, and accept and love ourselves as we are. As we do this, we will be able to go forth and love everyone more nonviolently.

Most of us are filled with conflict, division, and turmoil. We put ourselves down, and then put ourselves down again for doing that in the first place. Even if we want to be nonviolent to ourselves, we end up beating ourselves up over our failings.

The best way to reflect on our inner workings is to step back in quiet meditation and look deeply within. We can ask ourselves: "How am I feeling right this moment?" If we are cultivating

25

negative thoughts or feelings toward ourselves, we can gently acknowledge them, look at reasons or causes for these thoughts or feelings, let those thoughts or feelings go, breathe in the Holy Spirit of peace, re-center ourselves in the presence of the God of peace, try to accept ourselves unconditionally, and return to an attitude of nonviolence, love and care for ourselves. On bad days, this may be easier said than done, but if we attend to each of these steps, especially on bad days, we can claim our inner peace and cultivate inner nonviolence.

It also helps to take time in quiet meditation periodically to ponder our life journey. What violence did we experience from our parents, siblings, relatives, classmates or neighbors? How was this violence part of the larger culture of violence and war? How was our childhood, our youth, and our growing up influenced by the realities of violence?

What violence did we experience? How did we internalize it? How does that violence still linger within us? How can we let it go and move beyond it toward new feelings of peace, inner freedom and joy? These are great questions to ponder as we seek to understand ourselves and cultivate deeper levels of interior nonviolence.

If our parents did not shower us with unconditional love every single day, then at some level we likely learned that we are not worthy of unconditional love. We may not know how to show ourselves such nonviolent love. Psychologists teach that the first two years of early child development may be the most important in our lives. If we were not loved, affirmed, held, and blessed, then we may find it hard to love and affirm ourselves for the rest of our lives. This inner wound can eat away at us. Some turn to alcohol or drugs to relieve this pain, which only makes the situation worse.

If our parents did not show love to us, if our brothers and sisters beat us up constantly, if we suffered abuse at the hands of other school kids, if we grew up in a culture of war and violence, or if we suffered any type of discrimination because of gender, race, religion, nationality, ability or sexual orientation—at some level we probably internalized this hate and rejection. We were taught not to affirm or love ourselves, and so we may carry some level of low self-esteem. We likely carry this violence within and go through life feeling miserable and bringing misery to others. Worse, we end up taking out our pain on others—our children, our families, our co-workers. Some of us join the military looking for structure and purpose and end up channeling that inner violence onto the enemy—become trained killers and return home with unresolved experiences of war and new patterns of violence that wreak destruction in our lives and our families.

We were all raised in violence. We have all experienced violence. We have all suffered violence. We are taught that violence is normal, the way of the world, the way of life. We have no inkling that life could be otherwise. It is only natural that we internalize the violence done to us as children. If we do not explore and call out that legacy of violence, we will continue to do violence to ourselves and others. These unhealed inner wounds can breed hatred, resentment, anger, selfishness, misery, chaos and more violence. As we become more and more aware of what happened to us in childhood, we may begin to have compassion upon ourselves, accept ourselves, and be more nonviolent to ourselves.

Non-Cooperating With and Letting Go of Our Inner Violence

What can we do? As we recognize the wounds of violence within and the way we hurt ourselves, we can gently non-cooperate with that inner violence. This means, we try not to beat ourselves up and try instead to be more peaceful with ourselves. We show mercy to ourselves. We give ourselves a break. We remember that we are wounded victims of the culture of violence and that we are all in recovery. We take time every day to heal

27

ourselves, and patiently let the healing take its course, even if that healing takes decades or the rest of our lives.

As we begin to be kind to ourselves, we realize that it doesn't feel good to be violent to ourselves. Logically, we can realize the foolishness of hurting ourselves, of continuing the cycle of interior violence. So we need to ask ourselves throughout our day: *How am I feeling? Why do I feel down? Why do I have such hostile feelings within me and toward myself? How can I move beyond them? How can I cultivate more positive feelings within me and toward myself? What helps me feel better about myself and more peaceful, and how can I cultivate that inner peace so that one day it becomes my normal, daily experience?*

Often our deeply rooted, negative interior feelings are triggered because of what someone else has said or done. These encounters can trigger our childhood wounds, or other unresolved hurts from the past. So we need to recognize what has happened now and in the past, realize that we are continuing the cycle of self-abuse by beating up on ourselves, and choose instead to give ourselves a break, let it all go and breathe in the Holy Spirit of peace.

In this conscious self-awareness, the key is to let go of our inner violence, ideally, to give it to the God of peace. We tell ourselves: "I will not beat myself up. I will be kind to myself. I will have mercy on myself. I will understand myself. I forgive myself. I remember my wounds and my dignity and my commitment to the journey of peace and nonviolence. I choose to cultivate interior peace and nonviolence." If we can learn to let go of small negative thoughts about ourselves, we will eventually decrease the big negative thoughts about ourselves, and slowly over time, accept ourselves more and more, be more nonviolent to ourselves, and begin to create a place of peace inside us.

Some of us have grown so used to our inner violence that we might prefer it! We are comfortable with our self-hatred, low self esteem and inner violence. Changing our inner turbulence makes us feel uneasy. We're not used to inner peace. It feels scary, so we avoid it. We're used to inner pain, anger, violence, even rage. We don't want inner peace. This, too, has to be sorted out. We can recognize this trap as another mind game. We can let go of our fear and our delusional thinking that inner violence is "normal." We can risk inner peace and trust the good feeling it brings. We can let that new inner peace and nonviolence become the new norm, our new comfort zone.

Buddhist teacher Pema Chodron recommends "unconditional friendliness toward yourself." That's a lovely phrase, and seemingly easy enough. But as we start to practice unconditional friendliness toward ourselves, we may realize how little friendliness we actually show to ourselves. If we treat ourselves as our best friend, as a great person with immense dignity to be honored, respected, and cherished, we will begin to feel better about ourselves. Our inner violence will decrease and our inner nonviolence will increase. Then we will be better prepared to show that same nonviolence, love and unconditional friendliness to others. That means, trying from now on to act as conscious, nonviolent adults, not as wounded, terrified, violent children, victims of the culture of war.

Making Peace With Ourselves

The first step on the journey of nonviolence, then, is to make peace with yourself. To make peace with yourself requires showing compassion to yourself. If we want to show mercy, compassion, kindness and love to others, we have to show mercy, compassion, kindness and love to ourselves. For those who are not used to this, it can be a happy surprise to learn that it's more pleasant to be kind and merciful to yourself than to beat yourself up, put yourself down or go through life in total misery.

How can you be more nonviolent to yourself? How can you cultivate interior nonviolence more and more? Each one of us can answer that question in our own particular way. We can start with the basics and learn to treat ourselves well, take care of our bodies, get plenty of rest, exercise daily, eat only good, healthy food, spend time each day outdoors in nature, practice solitude, sit in silence, and keep a journal to reflect on our interior life so that we are aware of what's going on within us, what we are doing, and why we are doing it. This practice of taking care of ourselves over time will help us to be more conscious, feel more peaceful, and prepare us to respond peacefully to whatever crises will later befall us.

As we cultivate inner peace, we will begin to radiate peace around us. People will respond to our gentle, peaceful presence in a positive way, and that in turn will encourage us to love ourselves even more, be at peace with ourselves and deepen our inner journey to nonviolence. The deepening of our inner nonviolence, peace and love will lead to deeper outer nonviolence, peace and love.

I'm not encouraging us to be self-centered narcissists here, people unknowingly concerned only with our own selves. Unchecked egomania is simply another manifestation of low self-esteem, violence toward oneself, and little self awareness. Instead, I'm suggesting that true self awareness and heightened self consciousness leads to the reasonable practice of nonviolence towards oneself and greater nonviolent love toward everyone we meet.

There are many concrete daily steps we can take to help us with this inner journey toward peace. We can, for example, keep a "Violence and Nonviolence" journal, where we write down our memories and feelings of violence and wounding situations from our life journeys. We can also record memories and feelings of nonviolence toward ourselves, when we felt especially peaceful toward ourselves and how that affected our attitude toward others, and how we can cultivate such inner peace. We can list reasons for gratitude, inner peace and compassion toward ourselves, and write about how we can make such feelings more normative within us.

We can form or join a "nonviolence support group," some safe place where we can share the violence we have suffered and the violence we feel toward ourselves, as well as those breakthroughs of nonviolence toward ourselves and others. Also, we can meditate every day on our feelings of love, wonder and awe, give thanks for the blessings of life and peace within, and practice showing tender compassion toward ourselves within the light and grace of our nonviolent God. Such simple practices can make a world of difference within us. They can "reboot" the hardwire in our heads, transform our brain wave patterns of violence into new brainwave patterns of nonviolence, and create new nonviolent, physiological ways of peace that transform our bodies and our spirits.

Legendary peace activist Daniel Berrigan once wrote that whenever he had a particularly bad day, whenever someone was attacking him for his work to end war, whenever he grew sick and tired of himself, he sat down in quiet meditation—and pretended that he was an octopus. He would reach back with all eight of his arms and pat himself on the back many times over and over, saying to himself, "Good going kid! You're doing great! Hang in there! Keep at it! What a good person you are! God loves you!" Afterwards, he always felt better. That's the kind of self-affirmation we can begin to practice as well. Over time, as we care for ourselves, affirm ourselves, and make peace with ourselves, we will feel more empowered to love others and make peace with everyone.

All of this inner peace work is especially important for those involved in the public work for peace and justice. If we are not loving and affirming ourselves, we will be clueless as to the practice of nonviolent love toward others. I think the work of nonviolent resistance to the world's injustices and wars is extremely difficult because, among other reasons, the global issues of violence we are addressing can easily trigger the lingering violence within us and reopen our own past wounds.

31

Peacemakers, social justice advocates and activists need to be acutely aware of their own inner wounds and inner violence as they seek to address the world's wounds and violence. If we are not conscious about that connection, then we will often respond to the world's violence and need for peace from our inner violence, not our inner peace.

I have met many unhealthy, angry, mean, violent activists who stand for peace and justice, who seem to do more harm than good. They seem so passionate about the world's violence, but blatantly unaware of their own interior violence, so they act out violently to others. It's an old story, a common danger, an easy stereotype, but one that needs to be addressed and monitored as we pursue the path of nonviolence.

As we journey toward deeper inner peace and work publicly for peace, we do not want to do more harm than good! With all our good intentions, we do not want to end up hurting ourselves or others, much less turning everyone else off from the nonviolent struggle for disarmament and justice.

Conscious, self-aware nonviolence is the key.

Nonviolence begins with the conscious awareness that we are all victims of violence, that we are all wounded, and that we have all been indoctrinated in the culture of violence, so we need to tend to our own inner healing and try to learn how to become more nonviolent to ourselves and others. That personal, inner journey is the work of a lifetime; that's what the spiritual life is all about. We need to look deeply within and try to look at the causes of our violence and be gentle with ourselves and not beat ourselves up but cultivate interior peace and nonviolence. Then when we reach out to others and engage in the public struggle for disarmament and justice, with a real awareness of our own woundedness and our need for healing, we might actually help others heal and support the healing of humanity and the planet. We will know from our own inner experience what others are going through, and be able to teach them—because of our own good inner work—how to become true people of peace and nonviolence.

If we first tend to our own wounds, seek our own inner healing, and consciously walk the road of nonviolence one step at a time, we will help others to live the life of nonviolence. This inner work will help us heal the violence of others and start them down the road of nonviolence. If we consciously tend to ourselves, we may actually have a real gift of peace to offer others and the world. In this way, our lives will "bear good fruit," as Jesus instructs in his teachings on nonviolence in the Sermon on the Mount. We will be a gift and a blessing to those who meet us and to the world at large, and that's precisely what we all need—more gifts and blessings of peace.

33

3

The Daily Practice of Meditation
for Inner Peace

*When did you learn that you are the beloved son or daughter of the God
of peace?*

I often ask retreatants this question when we start a weekend
retreat. In our time together, we mull on a number of questions
that flow from this first one:

*How can you remember every day from now on that you are a
beloved son or daughter of the God of peace, and therefore a beloved
brother or sister to every human being on the planet?*

*How can you claim this core identity as a beloved son or daughter of
the God of peace more and more?*

*How can you live out more and more this fundamental truth even in
a world of violence and war, and go forth to love your sisters and brothers?*

*How is this realization disarming you and sending you forth to
practice creative nonviolence like Jesus?*

These are good questions to sit with.

Peacemakers throughout history testify to the need for quiet
meditation if we are to live the nonviolent life of peace. The story
of the nonviolent Jesus, according to Luke's account, begins with
him sitting in silent prayer by the Jordan River. In that quiet time
of contemplative listening and opening to the Spirit of peace, he
heard that he was God's beloved. In this sacred space, he was able
to take that message to heart, to claim that truth as the core of his
identity.

Like the nonviolent Jesus, we too need to sit still in silent
meditation and open our hearts and minds to the Holy Spirit of
peace and let the God of peace call us God's beloved. We need to
give God permission to love us, name us, and claim us if we want
to be disarmed, healed and freed to practice loving nonviolence.

That is why quiet meditation is so crucial to the life of nonviolence. In that silent meditation, we can hear God say to us, "You are my beloved." We learn who we are, we remember who we are, and we are strengthened once again to be who we really are. In that strength and confidence, we feel liberated from our inner violence and freed to get up and walk outside into the world of violence to offer the hand of peace and nonviolence.

After decades of experimenting with prayer, contemplation and nonviolence, I've come to learn that prayer—and life itself—are about our intimate relationship with the God of peace and love. Everything is about our relationship with God. If we can make our relationship with the loving God of peace a conscious priority in our hearts and day to day lives, we will become nonviolent people. It's as simple—and as hard—as that.

During those weekend retreats, I often ask people to recall the one person in their lives who loved them unconditionally. Maybe their mother, their grandmother, or their spouse. With that person, in that relationship, you knew you were loved, now and forever. Then imagine that God loves you a billion times more than that person. God loves each one of us personally, individually, unconditionally, wildly, infinitely. This is the truth of our lives.

Even though the churches rarely preach God's nonviolent love for us and its political implications for us, and the world of war mocks such spiritual talk, this truth remains true. That means prayer is not a duty or an obligation. In our prayer and silent meditation, we take time to sit in the presence of the One who loves us individually, unconditionally, in perfect peace. This is a good thing to do, a good way to go through life. It's comforting to be with Someone who loves you infinitely. It feels good to let God love us, heal us of our inner violence, and give us God's gift of peace.

The God of peace wants to love us unconditionally, with infinite kindness, but few people let God do this. This is the tragedy of the human condition. As we refuse to sit in the light of love, in the presence of the God of peace, we forget over time about God, and presume that God must be violent and warlike, like us. Then, we start to forget ourselves. We no longer remember our true identity and true purpose. We turn violent against ourselves and those around us. Our support for our nation's bombing campaigns, or the execution of a murderer, or racist or sexist policies, ultimately flows from forgetting who we are. We lose our nonviolence and in the process, our very humanity. We forget our relationship to our nonviolent loving God, and lose our faith, hope, and love.

Inner peace and global peace begin when we take quiet time to be with the God of peace every day. As we do, we begin to feel more peaceful with ourselves and to radiate that sacred peace with others. As we grow comfortable with this framework of nonviolence, we begin to understand who God is, who we are, and what life is about. This is a beautiful, healing process, and the hope for the whole human race.

Even if most people refuse this spirituality of peace, it remains true. God is so nonviolent with us that God allows us to freely accept or reject the way and wisdom of nonviolence. God leaves the choice to us.

I think the God of peace has been patiently waiting for us for our entire lives. It's like we're sleepwalkers, or we suffer from dementia and don't know who we are. If we dare wake up to reality, we can enter the presence of the God of peace and discover a whole new way of living—the way and wisdom of nonviolence.

Taking Quality Time Every Day to Dwell in the Peace of God

I recommend sitting alone in quiet contemplative peace with the God of peace for at least thirty minutes every day for the rest of our lives. Our personal relationship with the God of peace, with the One who calls you, "My beloved son, my beloved daughter," requires such quality time, as any intimate relationship does. In a marriage, if one partner speaks words of love yet the other partner never listens and never takes quality time be in that loving relationship, after several years, the marriage likely will die. The same is true with our relationship with God. If we don't take time to get to know God and be with God, how can we know God and be with God? Soon we give up on God and say we don't know God, that God is never with us. But God never gives up on us. God waits patiently to love us, to be with us.

Here, we discover how human God is. God wants to love us, be with us, and stay with us. All we have to do is show up and let God love us. God does the rest. The good news is that this feels good. It's better than sitting in pain, anger, hatred, bitterness, resentment, despair or violence. Every feeling, every emotion, every experience is transformed in the prayerful encounter with the God of peace. Like the crying child who runs to his loving mother's arm, we are welcomed with a loving embrace and feel comforted. We come away consoled, loved, strengthened, and ready for the next step. That's what happens in prayer. That's how to live the nonviolent life.

As we take time each day to let God love us, we begin to experience God as a loving, trustworthy, nonviolent parent. Over time, our knowledge of God changes because we have experienced God, God's love and God's peace directly. We know deep down to our very core that God loves us, just as that one person in our lives loves us unconditionally. In our daily prayer, we return to that love, feel that love, and find ourselves healed of violence because we are so overwhelmed by Love. The violence within us starts to dissolve and gets replaced by the love and peace of God. This is how God works: God's Holy Spirit of love gently disarms us, slowly transforms us, fills us with grace and peace, and somehow we find ourselves freed from inner violence to reach out in love for others.

We also begin to understand ourselves in a new way. We grasp Jesus' invitation to be the beloved sons and daughters of the God of love and peace. Over time, all our actions, work, relationships, and politics begin to reflect this peaceful "belovedness" from which we live out our lives. Like Jesus, we feel more peaceful and become peacemakers. We can help others discover who they are within the peace and nonviolence of God, and God's peace and nonviolence start to spread.

The spiritual practice of daily contemplative peace is good for our own sanity and healing. In this quiet prayer, as we dwell in the presence of God, and strengthen our relationship with God, God gently disarms our hearts and digs out the roots of war within us. In return God gives us the gift of peace. As we begin to become aware of God's disarming, healing work in prayer, and the new nonviolence we now feel, we can consciously join God's disarming process. We learn to bring all our inner violence, hatred, resentments, bitterness, anger and desire for revenge to the God of peace and give it all over to God, and welcome God's gift of inner peace.

This is a process that every individual ultimately has to figure out. It has to be lived. So my recommendation is: try it. Go to God, spend time in God's peace, give God all your violence, let God disarm your heart, and notice how you feel afterwards. I have found that I felt much more peaceful and whole after every encounter with God. That feeling of peace and wholeness is usually a good sign of an authentic experience of God's spirit working within and among us.

In this prayerful encounter, we learn that God would never hurt us, that God only wants to help us and to help every other human being. Our deeply conditioned violence blocks us from recognizing, feeling and accepting the fullness of God's unconditional, nonviolent love, which is why we need to return every day to this quiet prayerful encounter with God. Over time, our meditation helps break down our inner, learned barriers which block us from God's love. Gradually we feel God's love break through, touch us at deeper levels, disarm our innermost resentments and violence, and transform us in new ways.

It's in the safe confines of our prayerful solitude where we can say to our loving God, "Okay, because you love me, for your sake, I will try to be nonviolent to myself and love myself. I will forgive myself and accept myself as I am, just as You accept me as I am, warts and all." This daily mantra in the presence of God can open a new doorway to healing and inner peace.

Likewise, some of us may be filled with anger, hatred, resentment or bitterness to others, or a few key people in our lives. In the safe confines of our prayerful solitude, before the God of peace who loves us, we can look at our inner violence, allow the Holy Spirit of mercy and compassion to enter in, and grant clemency and forgiveness to those who have hurt us. As we forgive those who have hurt us, we begin to feel better. Our pain, anger, hatred, resentment and bitterness decreases, and a new spirit of peace rises within us. This is how the healing process works. If we do not take time in prayer to forgive and let go, that inner violence, resentment and bitterness will eat away at us. It will poison us and destroy us. It will boil over and lead us to act out with violence, even though in our right mind, we would never want to hurt anyone.

As we start to forgive those who hurt us, and deepen our intimate relationship with our loving God, we realize how much God has forgiven us. We become aware of the many times we have rejected God's love and peace, how God forgives and continues to love us, and how we can become even more forgiving and loving to those who have hurt us.

One way to engage the God of peace in our daily meditation is to read a few verses every morning from the Gospels (Matthew, Mark, Luke and John) during our quiet time. When I say read a few verses from the Gospel, I specifically do not recommend reading anything else. Do not read from the Hebrew scriptures or

St. Paul, or other parts of the New Testament, or even poetry or writings from the saints. If Gandhi is correct, that Jesus is the most active person of nonviolence known to history, and those of us who want to be people of nonviolence, like Gandhi, should get to know Jesus, study his life and actions, and try to emulate him. That can only happen if we are familiar with his story.

That's why I suggest a few verses from one of the four Gospels. Just sit with them in your silent prayer. Imagine what Jesus was like, what the situation looked like, and how he acted. Listen carefully to his exact words. Notice how he practices nonviolence. Ponder how he feels as he gets rejected or hurt time and time again, and yet how he continues to go forward in a spirit of nonviolent love. I think we are so far from the nonviolent Jesus that we Christians should spend about three or four decades with this daily practice of pondering the Gospels before we attempt anything else. We need to learn more about the nonviolent Jesus, discover how he did what he did, and try to catch some of his nonviolent spirit, if we want to join his campaign of nonviolence.

One other meditation practice that has helped me throughout my life is simply to sit in the presence of Jesus, and talk to him, and listen to him. This is an ancient Christian contemplative practice. Simply imagine being alone with Jesus. Look at him. What does he look like? How does it feel to be in his presence? How does he look at you? Listen to him. What does he say to you? What do you want to say to him? After you have spoken, stop speaking, and try to listen carefully. You may actually want to say, "Jesus, is there anything you want to say to me?"

In this simple conversation between friends, you get disarmed, healed, and liberated to be yourself in nonviolent peace. You can tell him anything, and ask his advice on everything, particularly about these core questions, feelings and struggles with violence and nonviolence.

Gandhi had only one picture in his room. It was a cheap, old reproduction of a sentimental nineteenth century painting of Jesus, knocking on a door, with a caption that read, "He is our peace." For Gandhi, that picture said everything. Over time, this becomes our experience, too: *Jesus is our peace.* He is our companion along the way, our teacher of nonviolence, and the very peace we experience in our daily silent meditation.

To be with the nonviolent Jesus in prayer is to experience peace and to become more and more like him, a person of nonviolence. In his presence, our violence evaporates, we cultivate interior nonviolence, and we discover ever new depths of peace. That's the spirit and feeling we want to live in for the rest of our lives, the spirit and feeling and reality we want to share with everyone we meet, indeed everyone in the whole world.

4

The Emotional Life of Nonviolence

A few years ago, my friend Nobel Peace Prize winner Mairead Maguire from Belfast invited me to join her at a unique gathering of ten Nobel laureates over several days in Denver, Colorado. Each laureate was invited to bring one friend or associate. Twenty of us spent three days together, as the Nobel laureates spoke to a stadium of some 10,000 people, an event open to the public; a gymnasium of 5,000 youth; and a hall with 5,000 local women. Another day was spent filming a BBC special conversation that was eventually seen by over a billion people worldwide.

At one point, the twenty of us were in the "green room," backstage at the stadium, waiting for the laureates to be called onstage. We were nibbling on the food, making small talk with one another. His Holiness the Dalai Lama and Archbishop Desmond Tutu of South Africa were sitting on a couch with the rest of us in a large circle around them. After a while, the conversation stopped. There we were, in a quiet lull, sitting together in silence. I was very moved to be in that circle. I felt consciously aware that this was a sacred moment.

"You know, Tutu," the Dalai Lama said in a voice loud enough for all of us to hear, "you are driving the whole world crazy. You have something to say about everything. Everyone wants to kill you. It might as well be me!" With that, the Dalai Lama grabbed Archbishop Desmond Tutu by the neck with both hands and started strangling him!

The rest of us were in shock. Before we knew it, Archbishop Tutu fell limp with his tongue hanging out of his mouth and his eyes closed.

Two seconds later, as if it had been choreographed, both of them fell on the floor, with their feet in the air, hands on their stomachs, mouths wide open—and tears rolling down their faces. They were laughing so hard, no sound came out!

Then, their laughter and tears and joy filled the whole room, and the rest of us started to laugh at these two big kids.

Just then, the stage manager walked in and said, "You're on!"

It was one of the most amazing experiences of my life. There on the floor lay two of history's greatest peacemakers, rolling around and laughing like children. They stood up quickly, brushed themselves off, walked onto the stage and spoke to thousands of people about peace, love and compassion.

"That's what I want," I said to myself. I'm tired of fear, anger, resentment, bitterness, ego, confusion and the violence that takes away my joy. I want what they have. I want to serve humanity, participate fully in the struggle for justice and peace, and live life to the full, which means, I want to laugh and—dare I say it?—taste the joy of peace.

I often recall this experience when I read the Sermon on the Mount. There the nonviolent Jesus gives specific instructions about what emotions to cultivate for the nonviolent life. He forbids anger and fear—and recommends grief and joy.

But wait—isn't that counter to everything we've been taught? We should be afraid! We should be angry! We should never grieve! And joy? You never hear the word mentioned in the mainstream culture—or even in the movements for justice and peace. It's as if no one knows what joy is anymore.

Somehow, many of the great peacemakers of history have learned these lessons. Yet they elude the rest of us. Take the two peacemakers I saw rolling around on the floor—Archbishop Tutu and the Dalai Lama. Both have been under constant death threat their entire lives. They have been faced with terrible violence and war. And yet, they are people of great joy. They are not known for anger or fear; they are known for their joy and for their sorrow. They exemplify the emotional life of active nonviolence.

43

The Way of Fearlessness

"For a nonviolent person, the whole world is one family," Gandhi wrote. "He will thus fear no one, nor will others fear him." For Gandhi, to be a person of nonviolence is to be fearless. You cannot practice nonviolence and be afraid. You have to overcome your fears; then you can go forward in love and confidence into the culture of violence and war with the message and work of disarmament and justice.

Jesus said the same thing. The one teaching he repeated most often in the four Gospels is straightforward: "Do not be afraid. Do not be afraid. Do not be afraid!" Jesus says it over and over again to his disciples. Obviously—they were terrified! At one point, he sends them out on a boat across the sea toward enemy territory as if to force them to deal with their fears. He, on the other hand, comes walking on the water in the middle of the night, as if to show that peacemaking—going into enemy territory to love one's enemies—is as easy as walking, even walking on water.

The Jesus portrayed in the four gospels was fearless. All hell seems to break out around him at all times. People clamor to touch him. His male disciples try to stop him and control him. The religious and ruling authorities endeavor to arrest and kill him—yet he remains calm and steady. He is fearless. Every moment of his life comes across as high drama, life-or-death, civil disobedience, yet he remains unflappable. Only in the moments before his arrest, a few hours before his execution, do we see him fall apart. In the Garden of Gethsemane, he breaks down weeping. But we're told, even there, he keeps his focus on God, starts praying, and soon regains his composure. He goes to his death in perfect nonviolence—what Gandhi called, "fearlessness." That's how he is able to say from the cross, "Forgive them; they know not what they do," and "Into your hands I commend my spirit."

If we live in fear, we will inevitably resort to violence to defend ourselves. As we institutionalize this fear in the culture of war, we stockpile weapons and tell each other to be afraid. Eventually, we reach for those weapons.

The way of nonviolence calls for an entirely different response and way of life. We no longer live in fear, so we do not stockpile weapons or resort to violent retaliation. Those who embark on nonviolence as a way of life come to grips with their fears. We name our fears, recognize them, reflect on them, and let them go. That means, we deal with every possible fear—loss of health, reputation, home, job, money, security, or family; or the possibility of arrest, prison, pain, and injury; and the inevitability of death. We let go of fear, and embrace the present moment of peace and the possibilities of love.

Gandhi insisted that the only way to live a life of nonviolence was to renounce every fear. In the early 1900s, while living on his community farm in South Africa, he decided to formalize his commitment to the life of nonviolence. So he professed a series of vows—a vow of poverty, a vow of chastity, a vow of respect for all religions, a vow of truth—and two key vows: a vow of nonviolence and a vow of fearlessness.

Gandhi taught that the presence of violence within us or the use of violence by us reveals our fear. It's much braver, more courageous, to live without fear and wage the struggle for justice without violence. This is a harder, more noble, more fruitful way of life. Gandhi spent the next four decades in the public eye fighting racism in South Africa and imperialism and terrorism in India without fear. He remained steady and peaceful, and kept his focus on the truth of the struggle and love for every individual, including his many opponents. He shows us that we do not need to live in fear, nor do we need to cooperate with the culture of fear.

"Nonviolence and cowardice go ill together," he wrote. "I can imagine a fully armed man to be at heart a coward. Possession of arms implies an element of fear, if not cowardice. But true nonviolence is an impossibility without the possession of unadulterated fearlessness."

How do we get beyond fear? Gandhi spent one hour in silent prayer every morning, and one hour in silent prayer every evening, communing with the God of peace. That prayer made the difference for him. If we root our day to day lives in our relationship with our loving God, if we continue to claim our core identity as a son or daughter of the God of love and peace, miracles will happen. We will find our fears slowly evaporating, and our confidence, love and joy slowly increasing. We will learn not to fear anyone, nor even to fear sickness and death, because we have come to know the God of peace and learned to trust God. We will know in the depths of our being that our survival is already guaranteed. God will take care of us, provide for us, and protect us.

What is there to be afraid of? We can go forth in a fearless spirit of nonviolent love toward every human being on the planet, and do our part to welcome God's reign of peace, justice and nonviolence. Fearlessness is a key ingredient in the nonviolent life.

Do Not Even Get Angry

But in the Sermon on the Mount, Jesus seems to up the ante even further. He not only forbids fear, he forbids anger. After the Beatitudes, he offers six antitheses. Each begins, "You have heard it said, but I say to you...." They lead up to his two most significant teachings which are the heart and core of nonviolence and Christianity: "Offer no violent resistance to one who does evil," and "Love your enemies and pray for your persecutors, that you will be sons and daughters of the God who makes his sun rise on the good and bad and causes rain to fall on the just and the unjust." But to reach those heights of creative nonviolence and universal love, we have to renounce every trace of anger and reconcile with those we have hurt.

The first antithesis states, "You have heard it said, 'Thou shalt not kill,'….but I say to you, do not get angry…" "Whoever is angry with his brother is liable to judgment…" Not only are we not allowed to kill, wage war, execute, or make nuclear weapons, we are not allowed to get angry! In some progressive circles, such talk is not only politically incorrect, it's downright infuriating. That seems to be exactly the point.

I remember once leading a small retreat for a group of older church workers, who had given their lives in the service to the poor. One woman blew up at this first antithesis. "This is ridiculous," she shouted. "Everybody gets angry, although I myself never get angry. Come to think of it, I am so angry at my mother, and at the church, and at all these teachings!" With that, she stood up and stormed out of the room. She was interested in the life of peace and the Sermon on the Mount, and though she claimed to be peaceful, her words and actions showed how far she was from peace. She was a wounded, angry, bitter activist, who seemed unaware of her unhappiness and the pain she brought upon others. She made life harder for everyone. We felt only sorrow and compassion for her.

Maybe Jesus was right. Maybe anger is a stumbling block to peace, love and nonviolence.

What if the nonviolent Jesus were at least as smart as us? What if Jesus' commandment holds a wisdom and way for peacemakers that could help us discover the same inner strength, calmness and peace that he knew? I think that's what he's trying to do—help us discover an interior peace and nonviolence strong enough to take on the world.

I do not imagine Jesus as a raving lunatic. I do not think of him as an angry person. I do not see him yelling or screaming at anyone, including the religious authorities. He could say strong words, but do it quietly, peacefully, firmly, like Gandhi or Thich Nhat Hanh. I can only find two moments in the four Gospels where the text says he felt "anger"—at the healing of the man with

47

the withered hand (Mark 1) and facing the fake mourners at the grave before he raises Lazarus (John 11). In both cases, the religious authorities were outraged at his speech and public healings, and eager to arrest and kill him. But actually, the Greek word used describes deep inner turmoil, more angst than anger. Jesus was more fed up, then enraged.

When he did his nonviolent civil disobedience in the Temple, it does not say he hurt anyone, or for that matter, yelled at anyone. We project that rage or violence on to him. As anyone who has done serious nonviolent direct action knows, you have to remain meticulously calm and peaceful if you want your action to be nonviolent. Jesus shows how well he understands nonviolence. In all of the accounts of his action, arrest, trial, torture and execution, he never blows up in a rage. He does not become angry. He keeps his soul. He remains at peace. He stays centered in his relationship with God. So he goes to his death in perfect nonviolence.

Even later, after all he'd been through, in the four accounts of his resurrection, there is no sign of bitterness, resentment, revenge or anger. He comes back with a gift of peace, makes breakfast for his friends, and sends them again on the mission of peace. As Daniel Berrigan once said to me, "Jesus didn't have a mean bone in his body."

In the Sermon on the Mount, Jesus pushes us to dig out the roots of violence, murder and war within us. Anger is the root cause of violence, he seems to say. We need to deal with it, its causes, and our response, if we want to live a nonviolent life. Jesus calls us to renounce killing, and the roots of killing within us—the anger that rises from our woundedness. He wants us to have not one drop of violence within us, to embody peace, love and compassion, even as we resist empire. That's why he urged us to rid ourselves of the roots of war, and war itself, all at once.

Anger is a neutral emotion. It comes from being hurt. If we are not mindful, we will act on that anger, retaliate with violence, and hurt those who have hurt us, maybe even kill, wage war or use nuclear weapons. Jesus is not telling us to repress our anger, which is our usual misinterpretation. That doesn't work. Sooner or later that repressed anger will come out. Rather, he urges us to deal with it, to channel that negative energy, through forgiveness and compassion into positive constructive work for the healing of others and the practice of creative nonviolence and universal love. And he gets quite specific about it.

Whenever you get stuck in anger, he says, remember those whom you have hurt, who have reason to be angry at you; then drop everything, go and be reconciled. *Katalgalete!* That's the Greek word: *Be reconciled!* That's the way out of the cycle of violence, anger, retaliation and despair—persistent reconciliation with everyone on the planet, starting with those we have hurt. Use your anger to remind you of all the harm you have caused. Channel your energy to heal the wounds you have caused.

"Therefore, if you bring your gift to the altar, and there recall that your brother has anything against you," Jesus teaches, "leave your gift there at the altar, go first and be reconciled with your brother, and then come and offer your gift...." Notice how Jesus speaks of killing, then anger, then worship, and then those we have hurt. He links topics most of us would never put together in one sentence. And yet it's true—murder, anger, hurting others, and worship are linked by our interior attitude. He wants us to cultivate an interior nonviolence, to be healed of our wounds, to forgive those who have hurt us, and to make atonement and reconcile with those we have hurt. In this way, we cultivate true interior nonviolence and let it bear good fruit.

To be reconciled means to apologize, say you're sorry, make restitution, offer gifts to those we have offended, and restore the right relationship of nonviolent love with others. For Jesus, this is a prerequisite for any worship. Only when we have reconciled with everyone we have hurt, can we approach the altar and offer true worship before God.

Apparently, God does not want our worship if we continue to hurt others, fester in anger, and cultivate violence. God wants nonviolence, compassion and reconciliation first; then God will accept our gifts at the altar. For Jesus, there is no true worship of God without justice, reconciliation, peacemaking and restoration of the human community.

Note, too, that Jesus does not advocate repressing our anger. On the contrary, he demands actively dealing with it, urgently addressing it. Its resolution takes priority even over our worship of God. He calls us to deal with our anger and violence right now, to take immediate steps to reach out to those we have hurt and to make this our first priority.

Gandhi read those words every morning and every evening for over forty years. He claimed the Sermon on the Mount held the greatest teachings on nonviolence in human literature, and since he wanted to be a person of nonviolence, he had to read from it, regularly, as a "how to" guidebook. After I learned this, I started to read the Sermon on the Mount more frequently, and to teach it. Over time, I noticed how specific Jesus' instructions are. They make up a catechism of nonviolence, the world's best compendium of peace. Gandhi took each sentence personally and tried to act on them. That's what Jesus wants for each of us.

"I have learnt through bitter experience the one supreme lesson to conserve my anger," Gandhi said at the end of his life, "and as heat conserved is transmuted into energy, even so our anger controlled can be transmuted into a power which can move the world."

"It is not that I do not get angry," he continued. "I do not give vent to my anger. I cultivate the quality of patience as angerlessness, and generally speaking, I succeed. But I only control my anger when it comes. How I find it possible to control it would be a useless question for it is a habit that everyone must cultivate and must succeed in forming by constant practice."

Anger will not sustain us for the long haul work of peace and justice. It may motivate us in the short term to get involved and take action. But it also stirs up the embers of violence within us and prevents us for deepening our nonviolence. We have seen this play out in recent decades as thousands of angry activists who marched, yelled and screamed—whether in the antiwar demonstrations of the 1960s or some of the Arab Spring demonstrations. Years of anger and rage eventually leads to burn out. People give up and walk away.

Instead, we need committed nonviolent activists who will struggle for justice and peace for the rest of our lives. That's what Jesus is teaching here. He is trying to form us to become lifelong practitioners of active nonviolence.

After thirty five years as an activist, I now know that that the more I learn about the world, the worse it appears. I can easily fall into rage, and its fallout—numbness, depression, and despair. What to do? I do not want to spend every day of my life in anger. That's no fun. That's not life-giving. And that's certainly not peacemaking. That's why I'm interested in taking Jesus at his word, and experimenting with his Sermon on the Mount nonviolence.

Likewise, when I ponder the great peacemakers I have known, such as Mother Teresa, Dom Helder Camara, Mairead Maguire, Daniel Berrigan, and Thich Nhat Hanh, I realize that they are not people of anger, but peace and joy. By all accounts, Gandhi and King, too, were not angry people. They laughed every day, told many jokes, and were known for their joy, even as they gave their lives for the struggle, and endured death threats. Folk singer and activist Joan Baez says that Dr. King was the funniest person she ever met. Such good humor is the mark of someone who has learned the lessons of the Sermon on the Mount.

Is it possible to conserve one's anger, to struggle for justice and peace throughout one's life, but to do so from a place of love and peace? I think so. I do not think Jesus would have commanded this teaching if it were not possible. I know that if I can maintain a daily practice of prayer and contemplative peace, and honor God's call to be God's "beloved," anything is possible. Even the cultivation of interior peace, joy and nonviolence. And so, with Gandhi, I recommend we pursue a new kind of "angerlessness," and cultivate revolutionary patience, steadfast nonviolence, passionate peacemaking, and a steady compassion for everyone. And in that spirit of inner peace, get on with the struggle of disarmament and justice.

Blessed Are Those Who Mourn

But Jesus surprises us even more. As he urges us to conserve the two common emotions of fear and anger, he recommends two other emotions which are rarely spoken about in today's culture of war: sorrow and joy. He recommends that we practice sorrow and joy on a daily level. This is what the Dalai Lama and Archbishop Tutu have taught me. As people of grief and joy, they model the nonviolent life.

The nonviolent person sees every human being on the planet as one's very sister and brother. That means, each one of us has over seven billion sisters and brothers! This is the truth of reality, the spiritual vision of peace. But in a world where thirty wars are daily waged, where one billion people starve and tens of thousands die each day from hunger and hunger-related illnesses, those of us who care for the human family are in shock. We grieve for all who die from poverty and war. In the last century alone, over 100 million people were killed brutally in warfare. We grieve for them. With the ongoing handgun violence, massacres, terrorist bombings, drone attacks, spread of disease, and the overarching threat of nuclear weapons and catastrophic climate change, we live in constant grief. We mourn for the dead.

Jesus teaches us to become aware of this need to grieve, and to make grief and sorrow a conscious, daily practice. In that way, we deal with reality, and find strength to go forward in loving nonviolent action. The action we take will come not from anger, but from a place of compassion, from our shared grief.

This is the exact opposite of what the culture of war teaches. "Do not grieve. Do not mourn. Do not cry," we are told. Two weeks after the September 11th 2001 terrorist attacks, President George W. Bush tried to stop the outbreak of national grief and compassion that was spreading. "Go shopping," he declared. Don't mourn; spend money. That's the message of the world of money, war and empire. And it makes sense: if you do not recognize the millions who are suffering and dying as your very sisters and brothers, then why grieve? Why be upset? And if you do not believe in the God of peace and love, then there's no meaning to life. "Why bother grieving? Go shopping, live it up, life is pointless," the culture of war and its spokespeople say. There may be short periods of grief for Americans who die, but no sustained grief for the countless sisters and brothers around the world who die unnecessarily. Only people of nonviolence, love and compassion grieve; those who support violence, killing and war dehumanize others and so they do not grieve.

The nonviolent Jesus begins his entire program of nonviolence in the Beatitudes with a call to be poor in spirit and mournful. "Blessed are those who mourn," he says, "they shall be comforted." Peacemaking, in other words, begins with grief. Peacemakers take time to grieve. I have friends, long-time nonviolent peace activists, who take quiet meditation time regularly to sit and grieve and weep over the suffering and death of the poor and those we have killed, and our treatment of one another and creation itself. They mourn and cry, and then having grieved, go forward to work publicly for disarmament, justice and peace.

This has to become a common practice among all those who pursue the nonviolent life. We need to make grief a regular part of our daily meditation. Grief needs to become a way of life for us. For the millions of impoverished people in the third world—from

El Salvador to Chile to Malawi to South Africa to India and the Philippines—this is an old lesson. The indigenous peoples of the world have long practiced grief. But wealthy first world people, especially North Americans, do not know how to grieve. We presume this is a morbid practice. In fact, it is a way toward healing and comfort, as those who care for the human family and the earth show us.

We all feel so helpless and powerless in the face of widespread suffering, daily violence and global destruction. If we take time each day to grieve the suffering and death of sisters and brothers, to grieve the violence around us and within us, to grieve the destruction of the earth, we will discover a new healing peace, as well as new strength to go forward on the path of nonviolence to do what we can to relieve human suffering and protect creation. That is one of the promises of the nonviolent Jesus: "They shall be comforted."

If we don't grieve, then we do not care about our sisters and brothers, or creation. If we don't grieve, then we are inhuman, and not nonviolent. The practice of grief allows the compassion within us to breathe and stretch, and the possibilities of universal love to grow within and among us. If we learn to grieve regularly, as Jesus recommends, we will awaken to our common humanity, expand our hearts, widen our compassion, and discover new horizons of peace. We will become, like him, people of genuine, all-embracing, universal nonviolence.

"Rejoice and Be Glad!"

But the good news is that Jesus does not leave us in grief. He calls us to rejoice! This too is an inconceivable concept for most North Americans, rooted in the angry, fearful culture of violence and war. Jesus clearly instructs those who struggle for justice and make peace to cultivate joy, especially to rejoice when they get in trouble for the work for justice and peace, which means every day.

"Blessed are those who hunger and thirst for justice," Jesus teaches in the Beatitudes. "Blessed are the peacemakers. Blessed are those who are persecuted for the sake of justice. Blessed are you when they insult you and call you every name on account of me: rejoice and be glad."

In Luke's version, the commandment is even more outrageous: "Leap for joy!" In other words, start dancing!

I think anyone who works for justice and peace should be filled with joy and dance regularly. I say this because anyone who works for justice and peace in a world of systemic injustice and permanent war will face constant persecution, harassment and trouble. The nonviolent Jesus urges us to turn this predicament around, and make it a cause for joy. We are provoking a reaction. The victory of justice and peace is imminent. Take heart, rejoice, leap up, dance, celebrate! This is the attitude of the Dalai Lama, Archbishop Tutu, Irish Nobel laureate Mairead Maguire, Gandhi and King. These great peacemakers are people of regular persecution and harassment, which is to say, they are people of great joy.

"Joy lies in the fight," Gandhi once said, "in the attempt, in the suffering involved, not in the victory itself."

How do we cultivate joy? How can we as nonviolent activists make room for joy? If we follow Jesus' teachings, first we can reflect on all the times we have landed in trouble for our work for justice and peace. How did we respond? Did we become angry, depressed or despairing? How could we have responded instead with joy, with love? Each one of us can reflect on the presence of joy in our lives, and in particular, the way we respond when faced with the political consequences of our public peacework. I hear Jesus urging us to be joyful, to cultivate joy within us, to find joy in our lives. Even as we face the most dire injustices and stare down the power of empire, and endure the greatest rejection, abandonment, even imprisonment, we can maintain an inner joy which the forces of death will never take away from us.

55

Once again, I believe that inner joy comes from the daily experience of dwelling in intimate love with the God of peace. We have touched the heaven of peace and joy that awaits us all. So while the struggle is difficult, the grief we feel immense, and our burdens heavy, we know a deep, inner joy that makes life worth living and defending. We know we are headed for resurrection, to a new place without violence, war or even death itself. We trust that with the resurrected Christ, nonviolence always wins out. So we go forward with full hearts, working for an end to war, violence and injustice, heralding the coming of God's reign of nonviolence.

If we want to live the nonviolent life, Jesus, Gandhi and the great peacemakers recommend that we let go of fear and anger, and cultivate grief and joy instead. In that way, we become more human, more peaceful, more compassionate, more loving. These recommendations may seem idealistic, utopian and unrealistic. But when one considers the alternatives of inner violence, anger, hatred, bitterness, and despair, one realizes that these teachings may be worth heeding.

In the end, Jesus taught, we have to become like children if we want to enter God's reign of peace. Children do not use guns, massacre others or build nuclear weapons. They live in the present moment of peace, feel their emotions, smile with love and rejoice in laughter. People of nonviolence become more childlike as they get older, as my encounter with the Dalai Lama and Archbishop Tutu demonstrates. That's the path that lies ahead for all of us— childlike wonder, unconditional love and boundless joy. These are the blessings of the nonviolent life.

5

Choosing to Live at Peace with Ourselves and the God of Peace

Nonviolence, when all is said and done, is a specific way of life, a conscious path. Before we move on to the second and third dimensions of the life of nonviolence, I invite you, dear reader, to pause and choose with me to live at peace with ourselves and the God of peace, from now on, come what may.

From this day forward, let's consciously choose to be nonviolent to ourselves so that we can become more nonviolent to everyone. Let's claim our identities as the beloved sons and daughters of the God of peace, plumb the inner, mystical depths of peace, and radiate personally the peace we seek politically and publicly for everyone.

Let's promise ourselves that we will no longer nurse violence within us or contribute to the world's violence, but spend the short time we have left on earth becoming the loving people of nonviolence we were created to be, and consciously spreading the way and wisdom of nonviolence in the hope that one day the world will become more and more a place of nonviolence, justice and peace.

From now on, let's become who we were meant to be, who we already are, like Gandhi, King and Day, people of loving, active, personal and public nonviolence.

This is a choice worth making, a path worth walking, a promise worth keeping, a good way to spend the rest of our lives. This, dear friends, is an invitation worth heeding.

Why spend one more moment stuck in the ditch of violence, riding along passively with the culture of violence and war? Let's start a new life, and begin and end each day for the rest of our lives in the Holy Spirit of nonviolence.

57

We can choose to live at peace with ourselves, to cultivate peace within us, if we want to. This is a choice we can make every day. Over time, it gets easier to choose a life of peace. As we let go of our inner violence and cultivate inner peace, we no longer cater to our mood swings, our violent tendencies, the culture's prejudices, righteous anger or desperate fears. We maintain a steady, even keel of peace. We become a rock of peace. In this way, our very presence pacifies others. While others are screaming, yelling, terrified and violent, we remain nonviolent, peaceful, centered in the God of peace.

Likewise, we choose to make peace with the God of peace. There are a million reasons to walk away from your local church or organized religion, but God remains peaceful, loving and nonviolent, and worthy of our attention, search and praise. We don't need to throw out the baby with the bath water. More than ever, stuck as we are in the culture of war and violence, we can seek the God of peace, open ourselves to God's presence, and listen for God's word of loving affirmation. We can turn to our Higher Power, ask God to disarm our hearts, and welcome God's gift of peace. We can try to do God's will of peace, take God's word of peace to heart and speak God's word of peace to the world of war. We can live in the light and peace of the God of peace if we want to. We need not be stuck in the darkness of violence and the culture of war. We can discover the truth of nonviolence which Jesus taught and the great peacemakers learned. We can surrender our hearts and lives to the God of peace, and begin the eternal life of peace—today.

This is another beautiful choice to make in a bad time—to make peace with the God of peace. As we do, we will receive many new blessings of peace.

These choices may require some changes in our lives. We will need to examine how we live, what we do, what our habits are, what makes us feel bad about ourselves, and what makes us more peaceful. We will need to take new steps to help ourselves feel more peaceful and become more peaceful. If we want to make peace with others, we will need to do our inner work of disarmament, learn to be at peace with ourselves and the God of peace, and cultivate inner nonviolence so that we will no longer spread violence in the world.

I invite us to take quality time every day in silent meditation with the God of peace, to get to know God, to let God love you unconditionally, and to fall in love with this loving God. As we sit in the silence of divine peace, we can let go of the violence within us, stop any self-abusive behavior, give our violence to God, allow the process of inner disarmament to play out, and dwell in the peace of God. As we lower our stress, let go of fear, resentments, and anger, grieve our losses and the death of the poor, we make room for joy, we let our hearts widen, we stretch out our compassion to embrace the whole human family. We open our hearts to the Spirit of God, and give God permission to use us for the salvific work of disarmament, justice and nonviolence.

Life is short. The world is full of violence and war. We can choose to spend our remaining time on earth in peace and nonviolence—toward ourselves, all others and all creation. To better make peace with others, to practice nonviolence toward others, we want to cultivate peace and nonviolence within ourselves. It's not an accomplishment; it's a journey, a lifelong, beautiful journey, full of blessings and graces that are ours for the asking.

One great fruit of our inner journey in God's peace will be a greater ability to be more nonviolent to everyone we know and meet. That is the second dimension of nonviolence which we turn to next.

Questions for Personal Reflection
and Small Group Discussion

How do you define nonviolence? What challenges you about nonviolence?

How are you violent toward yourself? How do you put yourself down, hurt yourself, cultivate inner violence and perpetuate violence, resentment and hatred?

Do you want to cultivate interior nonviolence and inner peace? How can you become more nonviolent toward yourself? What makes you feel violent toward yourself, and how can you move from inner violence toward inner nonviolence? Reflect on your entire life journey within the framework of violence and nonviolence. What do you learn about yourself?

Where is God in your life? What has been your experience of the God of peace? What is your image of God? How is God a God of peace and nonviolence? How can you make peace with the God of peace? What happens when you dwell with the God of peace? How have we experienced the peace and nonviolence of God? When did you hear God call you, "My beloved daughter" or "My beloved son"? How much quality time do you take with the God of peace every day? How can you spend more time with God every day? What does it mean for you to be a peacemaker, to be the beloved daughter or son of the God of peace, and to see every human being alive as a beloved sister or brother? How is God disarming your heart and giving you peace? Do you want God's gift of peace?

How is Jesus nonviolent and what does the nonviolent Jesus have to say to you these days about your heart and life? How is he inviting you to become more nonviolent, more peaceful, more loving? How can you become as nonviolent and peaceful as him? How can you follow his instructions on nonviolence in the Sermon on the Mount more and more? How do you live the beatitudes and love the enemies of your nation?

What are you afraid of, and how can you let go of your fears and move toward fearlessness, love and peace? What makes you angry, resentful or violent? How can you let go more and more of your anger, resentment and bitterness, move toward the healing of your wounds, forgive those who hurt you, reach out to those you have hurt, and try to reconcile more and more? What concrete steps can you take to cultivate "angerlessness," patience, love and compassion?

How can we grieve our losses and the death of sisters and brothers around the world? How can we make grief a daily contemplative practice of peace? How does conscious grieving lead to consolation and new energy to pursue justice and peace? How can we respond to rejection and persecution for our work for justice and peace with joy and gladness? How can we make more room for joy in our hearts and lives, and learn to rejoice over our justice and peace work?

How can we choose to be more nonviolent to ourselves from this moment forward for the rest of our lives? What changes are required for us to become more nonviolent here and now, and to practice nonviolence to others? How can we manifest a sincere commitment to the wisdom and way of active nonviolence for the rest of our lives? What do we have to do to become the people of peace we would like to be?

Part Two

Nonviolence Toward All Others

Nonviolence means avoiding injury to anything on earth in thought, word or deed.

— Gandhi

At the center of nonviolence stands the principle of love. To retaliate with hate and bitterness would do nothing but intensify the hate in the world. Along the way of life, someone must have sense enough and morality enough to cut off the chain of hate. This can be done only by projecting the ethics of love to the center of our lives. Agape love means understanding redeeming good will for all men and women, an overflowing love which seeks nothing in return. It is the love of God working in the lives of men and women. When we love on the agape level we love men and women not because we like them, not because their attitudes and ways appeal to us, but because God loves them. Here we rise to the position of loving the person who does the evil deed while hating the deed he does.

— Martin Luther King, Jr.

Living as we are in a time of emergency, thrown together in companionship with others of different races and creeds, let us try to think of ourselves as a community. Let us live in peace, and then we are a little oasis of peace in a war-torn world. Let us have no bitterness, no class strife, so that we can build up our strength to work for justice and love. Let us pray together, no matter what our faith is, for each other and for the whole world.

— Dorothy Day

6

Practicing Meticulous
Interpersonal Nonviolence

Virtually all of us have been brainwashed by the culture of violence to make some sort of armed peace through violence and to respond to violence with further violence. It's the way of the world: "An eye for an eye, a tooth for a tooth." But as Gandhi says, that just leaves us all blind and toothless—if not outright dead.

In the Sermon on the Mount, Jesus specifically addresses this cycle of violence, and commands us to break the cycle by refusing to retaliate with further violence. "But I say to you, offer no violent resistance to one who does evil." Love for neighbor, self and enemy was his antidote. These commandments of nonviolence bind every Christian to the way of peace. From now on, we non-cooperate with the downward cycle of violence, with the culture of violence itself. We are people of nonviolence, who reach out with active, generous, universal love, and we don't bite the hook of violence. We try to respond nonviolently at every moment in every situation to everyone. This is our spirituality, our way of life unto death.

Jesus offers specific examples about how to respond to violence with creative nonviolence. His life demonstrates a wide variety of nonviolent ways to respond to violence and to love every one by siding with the outcast and those in need. He is consistently provocative, publicly bold, and lovingly courageous. A disturber of the peace—that's Jesus, a disturber of the culture of war and violence. He's a revolutionary and a troublemaker, but he's always meticulously nonviolent. He remains nonviolent because he remains centered in his intimate relationship with his beloved God, claims his true identity, and keeps his soul in peace.

He invites us to maintain our inner nonviolence, our relationship with the God of peace, and to go forth into the culture of violence to be nonviolent to·everyone we meet.

As theologian Walter Wink astutely observed in his masterpiece, *Engaging the Powers*, the world says there are only two options in the face of violence: either run away and do nothing, or respond with further violence. Jesus, Wink teaches, offers a third way—where we do not run away, nor do we respond with further violence, but instead we stand our ground and actively respond with nonviolence, by insisting on the truth of our common humanity, loving our opponent, and using reason and creativity to disarm the person and lessen the violence. Jesus always brings peace, whereas the spirit of violence always seeks to escalate the violence. He insists that this is the way of God, that the Spirit of God cooperates with us when we attempt to resolve violence with nonviolence, and that this methodology can disarm us and be used to disarm the world.

If we make this methodology of nonviolence a way of life, then we will strive to relate to every human being we know and meet within this framework of Gospel nonviolence. We try to show respect, courtesy, kindness, empathy and compassion to everyone we meet. At the very least, we act with civility and decent manners, and affirm the dignity of everyone. Ideally, we try to show love for others and relate to others within the spirit of God's peace. But we do not hurt anyone. We bring no harm to others. We own no guns or weapons. All our actions, words, and attitudes flow from a positive, generous spirit of unconditional love, from an inner place of peace, from the mission of compassion and reconciliation, from the way and wisdom of Gospel nonviolence.

From now on, we practice meticulous nonviolence toward all others.

We try to be nonviolent toward everyone we meet in our ordinary day to day lives for the rest of our lives. We work to be conscious and mindful of our interpersonal nonviolence, to consciously cultivate an attitude of nonviolence toward everyone on the planet, and all creatures and creation itself.

You might say this sounds easy, but there's a reason we're so violent. Nonviolence is hard; violence is easy. We're used to violence. It's so deeply rooted within us that sooner or later it always rears its ugly head. We go along with it because it's second nature. We're constantly provoked, and rarely encouraged to be nonviolent.

Though nonviolence is hard, it's actually not quite as hard as violence. Violence hurts everyone involved—its victim and its victimizer. It brings pain of all kinds, including physical injury and death, but also emotional, psychological and spiritual pain. It never leads to the consolation of the Holy Spirit. It always leads to despair, hard feelings, resentment, bitterness and worse.

Nonviolence, on the other hand, does not hurt the other person. It's hard to practice, and may require that we accept suffering in pursuit of the truth with love without resorting to violence, but it heals even as it works. It takes time and requires patience, but it always leads to the consolation of the Holy Spirit. It can lead to new hope, forgiveness, justice, reconciliation and transformation. And those should always be our goals.

Nonviolence All Around

So first of all, as people of meticulous interpersonal nonviolence, we will be nonviolent toward our families, our spouses, our children, our parents, and those close to us from now on. The days of domestic violence, spousal abuse, child abuse, and parental abuse are over. We can't pretend to be nonviolent if we are hurting those around us.

Gandhi once told an activist that when you start to practice nonviolence, it does not affect the King of England; it first affects those around you—your family and friends. That's where you have to begin your attentive interpersonal nonviolence.

And that's where the rubber hits the road. Whether it's coming up against long held resentment toward our parents for violence done to us in childhood, or hurt feelings and anger toward our spouse, or shot nerves from the crying baby who tests our patience—nonviolence begins at home. It gets tested up close. These tense situations give us the chance to practice nonviolence and to grow in compassionate love. We can transform them into new opportunities to show God's nonviolence.

We possess the tools of nonviolence, so these moments provide us with the opportunity to use our tools. We can learn through these specific situations not to retaliate with violence, or to submit meekly to violence. We can experiment with dialogue, listening, sharing, prayer and every nonviolent means possible to maintain our peace and create ever more nonviolent relationships. If we are going to be sincerely nonviolent, we have to be extra attentive to our feelings with those around us, and expend extra energy to create a community of nonviolence with those around us.

We need to reflect seriously about how we can be nonviolent to those closest to us, especially those who have hurt us or those we have hurt. Families in the U.S. have become so shockingly dysfunctional because of this cultural plague of violence that this is no easy task. In some cases, the nonviolent response may be to withdraw involvement from a violent family. We certainly do not want to let the violence of controlling, domineering, unloving relatives determine our lives or prevent us from getting on with the salvific work of peace.

In any case, we need to reflect about our close relationships within the framework of violence and nonviolence and do what we can to decrease the violence, increase nonviolent awareness, and grow together in loving kindness and peace. We want those around us to feel peaceful and well loved; our goal should be to create relationships of nonviolence in every aspect of our lives.

In particular, we have to shower every child around us with unconditional, nonviolent love, encouragement and affirmation. No more violence, no more yelling, no more put downs. The days of child abuse need to come to an immediate end, starting with us. As we love and encourage our children, teach them nonviolence and model nonviolence for them, we sow the seeds for a future generation of peace. Besides, it's enjoyable to make children and those we love happy. And it's consoling to show them and teach them how to be nonviolent, knowing that they will grow up with a better chance of inner peace and a nonviolent life.

I have seen this work among countless families around the world—with long time activist parents, to inner city church families, to Salvadoran refugee families in displacement camps. The ideal of unconditional nonviolent love among families is possible. It requires talking, dialogue, cooperation and compromise, a committed process of working through our disagreements and differences in an ongoing, conscious conversation that stays attune to the pulse of the relationship or family spirit. If we help each other practice nonviolence, affirm and encourage each other, anything is possible.

In her great book, *Taking the War Out of Our Words: The Powerful Art of Non-Defensive Communication*, Sharon Ellison outlines several ways to communicate nonviolently using non-defensive approaches. In contrast to what she calls the "war model" of communication—an approach that uses defensiveness for self-protection and power struggle to achieve our goals, a model most of us are consciously or unconsciously schooled in from the time we are born and that often "undermines our ability to achieve our goals and creates much needless pain in our lives" by waging conflict through counter-attack, surrender or avoidance—she proposes a dramatic alternative.

Ellison reframes our typical three communication tools—asking questions, making statements, and making predictions—from weapons of war to tools for gathering accurate information, speaking with clarity, protecting ourselves, and holding others more accountable. "The outcome is that we can be direct and honest, open and transparent, gaining integrity while keeping spontaneity," Ellison writes. "We are more likely to feel compassion for others, while having the capacity to create clear boundaries. We can build the kind of character that enhances our own creativity and success, while prompting others to have greater respect and caring for us." Her work, along with other teachings on nonviolent communication, can help us sustain nonviolent relationships.

Then, there are the people in our workplace. If we are going to be nonviolent, our livelihood has to come from life-giving, not death-dealing, work. We can't work for the military, or a weapons manufacturer or a gun maker. Within this life-giving workplace, we want to be fair, just, kind and friendly. We do our best to be nonviolent to everyone on the job, to be part of a team, to help everyone discover new depths of peace while doing work which serves others. This requires placing a higher value on our humanity, on service, on nonviolence and the common good, rather than on profits, ego or honor. If any aspect of our work contradicts the nonviolent life, then we need to quit and move on to work that is nonviolent and life-giving.

If we are part of a church or religious community, we likewise want to maintain our nonviolence toward every one. A church or a religious community is supposed to be, first of all, a community of nonviolence. Given the violence of the world, and the church's frequent silence about war and nonviolence, we need to help our local church become more nonviolent. It's no use going to church every Sunday to hear sermons which uphold American warmaking and personal greed, and leaving angry or more entrenched in the culture of violence. Church life should make us more nonviolent, loving and peaceful.

We need to help Christian churches become training camps of Gospel nonviolence, where we learn together about the violence within us, ponder the commandments of nonviolence, dwell in God's intimate love, deepen our relationship with Christ's community of peace, and feel strengthened to go forth into the world of war on the mission of peace. The church should help us live the nonviolent life: that's what the nonviolent Jesus wants! If it's not fulfilling this mission, we should push it to meet its purpose, or find another more peacemaking community.

If we're part of a local peace and justice group, or join a public protest, or even engage in a civil disobedience action, we need to be especially, meticulously nonviolent. How can we espouse nonviolence publicly for the world, if we are cruel, mean, or abusive to those who care about humanity and the world? Interestingly, peace and justice groups are usually comprised of opinionated, strong-willed, vocal people, those who push our buttons, push their own egos, and push others around. We do not want to be pushy like that. We want to model nonviolence in our peace groups as we prepare to push publicly for peace with justice.

Then, there are ordinary people we meet as we go through our day to day lives—at the grocery store, the gas station, on the bus or an airplane, as we're walking down the street or sitting in the park. We want to be nonviolent to everyone. We want to be especially, intentionally nonviolent to those in need—the marginalized, homeless, outcast and hungry. We try to make a preferential option for the poor and disenfranchised, to help and serve those in need as best we can, to affirm and encourage everyone on their journey toward peace.

I have an activist friend who greets everyone he meets as he walks down a street as a beloved brother or sister. He has a radical political critique of the world but an eternally sunny disposition, and tries to connect positively with every human being he encounters. I wish I was like that. I am not like that by nature. My friend has taught me much about being nonviolent and generous. I want to interact with others in that same generous spirit. If I am stressed, busy or tired, I easily become impatient, even grouchy,

71

and that affects my attitude in those ordinary day to day encounters in a negative way. I recall my commitments and my desire to be friendly and nonviolent.

These days, I try to practice nonviolence in small encounters so that I'll be better able to respond nonviolently when the big moments suddenly come along. I do not claim any heroism or special gifts of nonviolence. I am as violent as everyone else because I am a product of our culture of violence and war. But I do claim to be called, like everyone else—to become nonviolent, to reclaim my true self, and to be nonviolent to everyone I meet, even to love my neighbor and my enemies, to radiate personally the peace I seek politically. I want to follow the nonviolent Jesus, and that means doing my inner work and public work of personal disarmament and active nonviolence. That's a worthy struggle for all of us.

Life is short. I believe we are headed to a new heaven of nonviolence that longs to come to earth now. When we get to heaven, we will wish that we had used our time on earth more wisely to love others, to be nonviolent, and to help spread peace as opposed to continuing the cycle of violence and war. The challenge is to enter that awareness now and to use the short time we have left to be as loving, disarming, nonviolent and peaceful as possible. Toward everyone. From now on!

"Choose nonviolence. Practice nonviolence. Love everyone around you. Make peace." Those are the standards of the peacemaker. That is the message of Martin Richard, Martin Luther King, Jr., Dorothy Day, and Mohandas Gandhi. Even if we can't reach those noble heights, the struggle to be nonviolent is itself a victory for love and the God of peace. It is the only struggle worth pursuing.

7

Nonviolence Toward Those
Who Are Violent To Us

Gandhi used to say that it is not nonviolence if we are merely nonviolent to those who are nonviolent to us. True nonviolence, "the nonviolence of the strong," he called it, comes when we pit ourselves against those who do violence to us or others. If we can intervene, disarm and convert others to the truth of love and peace through our creative nonviolent action, then we practice authentic nonviolence. The test comes as we insert and maintain our nonviolence with those who are not nonviolent, and actively try to disarm and heal them. If we are able to disarm and change them, wonderful; if not, at least we tried, and through our nonviolence, caused them no further harm. But we cannot sit by and remain passive with those who are violent. If we do, then we are merely cooperating with violence.

Everyone knows someone who is not nonviolent to them. It could be anyone—a parent, a sibling, a child, a spouse, a distant relative, a neighbor, a boss or someone at work. What do we do? Every situation, every incident, every person is different. We can reflect deeply on the situation, pray for those involved and for guidance, and try to respond as best we can. Through our creative nonviolence, we try to win them over with our loving kindness, disarm them, heal them and become friends. As we respond with loving nonviolence toward those who are not nonviolent, we remember that the God of peace is with us both, blessing our journey toward disarmament and peace.

Some people carry so much emotional baggage with them that they are not able to lighten other people's loads. My grandmother used to refer to those who are not easy to be with, who make life harder, as "difficult people." How do we relate to them, how do we help them, how do we love these "difficult" people? Nonviolently! With as much love, compassion and wisdom as we can muster. In the process, we recall that we too can be "difficult," and that remembrance helps us to show compassion toward them. The key in every relationship and encounter is to maintain our nonviolence, help others deepen their nonviolence, and grow in peace, hope and love.

One of the greatest practitioners of interpersonal nonviolence is Saint Therese of Lisieux. Though she died at the age of 24 in a cloistered Carmelite monastery in France in 1890, she became a spiritual master in the art of nonviolent love toward those around her, especially the most miserable and unpleasant. Her autobiography—one of the most widely read spiritual classics in history—records her experiments with unconditional nonviolent love towards the sisters in her community. She waged assertive nonviolent love toward everyone, especially the bossy superiors and bitter elderly, until she wore them all down. She tested Jesus' way of nonviolence and found over and over again that it works.

Her attitude toward Sister St. Peter provides a good example. Poor Sr. St. Peter was confined to a wheelchair, and was as mean and nasty as could be. No one liked her. Young St. Therese was periodically assigned to care for her, and made up her mind to respond to every nasty remark with a gracious smile and a kind word. Just before Therese died, the elderly sister confided in her that she was the only one in the monastery who was nice to her. Therese had won her over, and made a new friend, but grieved the other sisters' failure to love unconditionally. This practice of unconditional nonviolent love was hard for Therese, even in a monastery of cloistered nuns, but she practiced it diligently and through her writings, converted them all to what might be called "the little way of nonviolence." Her nonviolent love models the Christian response of nonviolence to all those we meet, especially the most "difficult."

As we reflect on our nonviolence, we can ask ourselves: who are the people who trigger our violence, our resentment, and our hatred? Whom do we not love, do we not want to be nonviolent to? How do we make peace with them? Who has hurt us, whom do we want to hurt, whom have we hurt, and how can we transform these situations? Of course, we're all for peace, I tell people in my talks, but deep down, there's usually someone we'd really like to get even with—whether a president, a pope, a general, a boss, a parent, a sibling, a neighbor, or a co-worker. Often there's at least a trace of vengeance lurking within.

Someone always triggers our violence. What do we do? We make them our teachers. They expose our inner violence to us. They show us what Carl Jung called our shadow side—the unconscious, least desirable aspects of our personality that we often project onto someone else. Our response to them measures our nonviolence. If we can't respond nonviolently to them, we will not grow in the practice of Christian nonviolence. So we need to pray for them, pray over the situation, ponder what's going on inside them, learn what brought them to their violence, and explore creative nonviolent responses. Such reflections will open new wells of compassion within us, and enable us to show new depths of merciful love that can heal them.

In his book, *Personal Nonviolence: A Practical Spirituality for Peacemakers*, Gerard Vanderhaar offers this concrete advice:

> Loving a difficult person nonviolently means first of all putting aside notions of winning. It is especially important, in working it out, to avoid self-righteousness and the kind of moral pressure that humiliates the other side. We recognize their weakness, embarrassment, and fears, as we acknowledge our own. Real progress comes from giving the other side options to respond to, not demands to be met. People react poorly to ultimatums. They generally become defensive and hardened in their positions. Through patient perseverance in loving, not necessarily

liking, difficult people, we have a good chance of finding a way to live in harmony, respecting their humanity while being true to our own. (Wipf and Stock, 2013 edition, p. 59)

Psychology helps us to understand how others were hurt and unloved as children, how they have not been taught to be loving or peaceful, and how stuck they are in old patterns of violence. Indeed, everyone is damaged by the culture of violence to some degree. We can love them, show them compassion and remain nonviolent to them, and perhaps through our human response, help them heal a little. This is part of the nonviolent life.

But nonviolence does not mean staying in abusive relationships, or putting up with domestic violence. Nonviolence demands a refusal to be hurt or abused or humiliated, just as we refuse to hurt, abuse or humiliate anyone ever again. If someone you know humiliates you, abuses you, and practices violence towards you, tell them to stop. If that doesn't work, try again. Then, according to Civil Rights leader and teacher of nonviolence Diane Nash, we should break from that person so that we no longer suffer such personal humiliation and violence, and also so that person does not continue the practice of humiliation and violence. We do not want to let them hurt us, nor do we want to hurt them.

Sometimes, if we stay with people who cause us pain, it only hurts us further. In that case, we need to examine our co-dependent tendencies, and perhaps attend an Al-Anon meeting for support and insight into our behavior. No one should remain in an abusive relationship. Nonviolence means ending all abuse and humiliation, so that there is no longer an abuser and an abused person, an oppressor or oppressed person, a victim or victimizer. Through our global peace movements, active nonviolence seeks to end the violent abuse of one nation upon another or others.

Sometimes the feelings of resentment, bitterness and anger toward those who hurt us linger for years afterwards. Those inner feelings of violence or rage need to be addressed. Allowing them to simmer is not the way of nonviolence either; one day they will likely boil over in an outburst of rage and violence. Sooner or later, we need to drop our anger, resentment and bitterness. We need to forgive those who hurt us, and make forgiveness a regular practice in our relationships so that we can cultivate nonviolence within ourselves and among all those we know. We want to give our hard feelings to the God of peace, forgive everyone, receive God's forgiveness and merciful love, and cultivate an interior peace, so that we can maintain peaceful relationships, cultivate new ones, and go forth publicly as true peacemakers.

All of this growth in nonviolence toward those we know can help us for the day when we stand up publicly for justice and peace. When we do stand up, speak out, and take nonviolent public action for justice and peace, we need to be prepared for a negative response, a hostile reaction. Given our culture of violence, some people will object to our stand, our protest, our nonviolent action. Usually, those are the people closest to us, starting with our families, co-workers, church members, and neighbors. Some of them will confront us. They might get angry, they might yell at us, they might denounce us, they might call us every name in the book. All of this is to be expected if we take a public stand for justice and peace in a culture of permanent injustice and war.

What do we do? We need to be prepared. How do we respond? Nonviolently! When someone denounces us for our peace and justice stand, it does not help to shout back, denounce them or be violent. It helps to listen, to let them speak, to allow them to let off steam, and to accept that heat without retaliation. Remain calm, quiet, attentive, compassionate and peaceful. We may not get the chance to convince them of our position, but our nonviolent response may touch them and inspire them in ways we'll never know. Clearly our stand has already touched a nerve with them, so our nonviolent response will nurture the truth that they recognize deep down, perhaps even at a subconscious level. A calm response often shames people into recognizing their wrong-headedness and violence. In that moment, they may recognize themselves, and choose the peace that they meet in us.

There are remarkable photos of the 1963 Birmingham campaign showing Martin Luther King, Jr. listening intently to the notorious Police Chief Bull Connor and other racist opponents. Dr. King's steady calm response demonstrated his consistent nonviolence, and exposed the violence of the racist establishment leaders. It also inspired the thousands who came out to demonstrate. They saw in Dr. King's personal stand that it is possible to remain nonviolent literally in the face of our violent opponents. They witnessed the courage, dignity and moral grandeur of Dr. King's position. They learned that personal nonviolence always has an effect. If we respond to our violent opponents with violence, we will only continue the downward cycle of violence. But if we dare practice loving, thoughtful, calm nonviolence, we will touch, heal and inspire others. Our nonviolent response will bear good fruit, maybe not immediately, but eventually. This is one of the promises of the nonviolent Jesus.

Shortly after the attack on the World Trade Center on September 11th, 2001, I joined with two dozen friends in an anti-war protest in Union Square in New York City. It was a beautiful, Saturday afternoon which had brought out tens of thousands of people to the park to enjoy the city, look at the artwork for sale, buy organic food, and listen to musicians. In their midst, we stood, holding banners that read: "Don't bomb Afghanistan!," "Practice Nonviolence," and "Live at Peace with the World."

Holding one of the banners, I stood in the center while Fr. Daniel Berrigan stood at my right and our friend Fr. Bob Keck stood on the left. Half way through our one-hour silent vigil, a large young man who looked like he might have once been in the military stormed right up to me, emphatically pointed his finger at me, and started yelling, "How dare you protest our government!

Go back to Russia where you belong! You would let all the terrorists of the world invade our great country and kill us all!" He was livid. His eyes were bulging, and he screamed at the top of his lungs. Then, he looked me in the eye and said, "What would you do if I pulled out a knife and killed you right now?"

I had just come from the Family Assistance Center on 47th Street, where I served as a Red Cross coordinator of 550 chaplains ministering to some 50,000 direct relatives of the victims of the 9/11 attacks. I took a deep breath, looked him in the eye and said, "I guess I would die and go straight to heaven, and be with Jesus, Mary and the saints and live forever at peace. You, on the other hand, would be arrested and charged with my murder. There would be a big public trial, and you would go to prison for the rest of your life and always regret killing me. I would feel very sorry for you, and so would my friends. We would pray for you."

He was stunned. For the first time, he was speechless. I guess he expected me to shout back, denounce him, and start a fight. But my talk about my death, my ascension to heaven and his descension into prison knocked some sense into him. He looked down at the ground, swallowed hard, and walked away. One of the Catholic Workers in our group approached him and started to explain our peace vigil. Bombing Afghanistan will not end terrorism, he said calmly; it will only kill more people, inspire more people to become terrorists, and lead to more terrorist attacks against us. After awhile, the young man walked back over to me. I'm sorry I yelled at you, he said. He put out his hand and I shook it. Somehow an explosive moment was diffused, and we maintained our nonviolence.

How do we respond to those who threaten us with violence? Nonviolently! If we respond with similar anger or violence, we can be sure that we will receive the full brunt of his promised violence. If we respond with reason, insight, wisdom, humor and creativity, using the methods of Jesus and Gandhi, we might disarm the opponent and make a new friend.

In all things, be nonviolent. In all relationships, be nonviolent. In all protests, in all encounters, in all confrontations, be nonviolent. Train and practice nonviolence in those small, tense, day to day encounters with those around you that you might develop muscles for later on, so that you can practice the "nonviolence of the strong," like Gandhi and Dr. King.

Every encounter provides an opportunity to experiment with the way of nonviolence, to test our nonviolence, and to grow so that we can become authentic peacemakers, real practitioners of nonviolence in a world of violence.

8

Joining Local Circles of Peace
and Nonviolence

As we practice personal and interpersonal nonviolence, and love ourselves and all those we meet and know, we widen the circles of love and peace around us, and create more and more circles of love and peace that will spread far and wide. We try to be as loving and compassionate as we can, let go of our hurts and resentments, forgive everyone who has hurt us, try to outdo one another in kindness, and build friendship with every human being we know and meet. This simple process of love builds community. Being part of a community of peace is what it means to be human.

These circles of peace, love and nonviolence widen, touch others, and envelop one another like ripples that keep rolling beyond us and touch everyone in the global pond. In this way, we build up the global beloved community of sisters and brothers. We help each other become we who truly are—the beloved sons and daughters of the God of peace and love.

I've tried to do this over the course of my life, to reach out to everyone I've met and to make new friends, as many friends as possible. Once they get a taste of my political work for disarmament and justice, some turn away. But many others join my circle of peace. I've lived all over the country and traveled the world extensively, so after many decades, there are many circles of peace in my life. Together, we become a grassroots movement of peace, love and nonviolence. It's unseen and unknown, but an organic reality.

In 1992, for example, I helped start twenty-five little peace groups throughout the San Francisco Bay Area, some of which continue to do this day. All these friends make life rich, busy, exciting—and hopefully will bear the good fruit of peace. Of course, I've made many mistakes. Friendships end, groups break up, people come and go. Nonetheless, it's a beautiful journey—to go through life building circles of peace, love and nonviolence around us that connect with other good people in the hope that we might model and build up the beloved community we seek. In the end, we transform the world from a place of armies, corporations, nations and empire, into communities within communities within ever-widening communities of peace. I think that's what the God of peace intended for us.

Change comes from the bottom up, never from the top down, no matter how hard we insist that top down organizing works. As we build relationships of peace and nonviolence, we strengthen this grassroots movement that can subvert the systems, structures, nations and empires which oppress and kill humanity. Along the way, we sow seeds of love and nonviolence that one day can bring a new harvest of peace. Through these circles and communities of peace and love, we can do more, touch more, and reach out to more people than we imagine. The Spirit of peace, it seems, is unleashed more broadly when we work in community than when we work alone.

This is certainly the story of the nonviolent Jesus. One of his first steps in each Gospel account is to form a community around him. Apparently, he knows that he can do more good with others around him, and that his public work for justice, healing, and peacemaking will touch more people if he is getting the support he needs, and if he supports others to carry on his mission. Historians suggest that the development of the small community of nonviolence and resistance, which describes the nature of the network of the early church, eventually helped bring down the Roman Empire. It remains a model for us today.

It's also the story of Gandhi. He spent nearly fifty years living in an intentional community of nonviolence, which at times had as many as 400 members. A few years ago, I traveled with Arun Gandhi, his grandson, and other friends, to visit Gandhi's community ashram in Ahmedabad. I was deeply moved to be in the house where he lived for twenty years, where he spent two hours a day in meditation, where he and his friends discerned their lifelong campaign of nonviolence. In various biographies, community members later spoke of the contagious joy they felt in Gandhi's presence. He was someone that people gravitated to. It was his vision, his life, his spirituality, his peaceableness. Hundreds, thousands, millions flocked to be near him. In the community, they shared everything in common. His wisdom, peace, and good cheer easily rubbed off. They took turns cleaning up and cooking for one another, living in voluntary poverty, and preparing to resist British imperialism with their very lives. Nonviolence was their "creed." Together, they encouraged one another to give their lives not only to the nonviolent life, but to the vision of a new world of nonviolence. They dreamt an impossible dream and helped make it more possible. In some ways, Gandhi's powerful nonviolence touches more people today than ever.

For decades I lived in community. I learned that if people get along, give each other space, support each other's work, pray together, and share a common spiritual vision, community life can be invigorating and rewarding. It holds definite responsibilities, as any way of life, but also infinite possibilities. But whether we live together in community or meet regularly with like-minded peacemaking friends in community, I came to the conclusion that community is only experienced in occasional "moments." It's something that we have to keep working at, showing up for, and journeying towards. As with everything, the expectations of every community member need to be addressed regularly so that common ground can be shared. But it is a goal that makes life far richer, and our work far more fruitful.

These days, we don't necessarily need to live in a community house with others, but we can join a local peace and justice community that meets once a week or every other week. When we participate in little peace groups, we find that we are not alone.

There are other like-minded friends with whom we can share our concerns, fears, hopes and frustrations. Together, we can pray, study, read, discuss and then plan a public witness for peace and justice. In the process, we find ourselves strengthened to live a more nonviolent life, and we help one another deepen our experience of nonviolence. More, as we stand up publicly together, we can help transform our local neighborhood or city or state or nation. Through small local communities, everyone can experience the power of grassroots nonviolence and spread the circles of nonviolence.

Across the country, these circles of peace and nonviolence are quietly spreading. In Washington, D.C., friends at the Catholic Worker and Church of the Savior serve the poor, maintain regular peace vigils at the Pentagon and White House, and network with many other groups and peace activists. In Los Angeles, the Catholic Worker and Office of the Americas keep the work of peace alive. In New Mexico, Pax Christi friends have maintained an annual nuclear disarmament vigil at Los Alamos for years, trying to lift up the vision of nonviolence. In Baltimore, the Jonah House and Viva House communities have spoken out for peace and justice for decades. In New York City, a small group called Kairos, has been meeting every two weeks for four decades, and organizing regular demonstrations, campaigns and public witnesses that have touched countless lives. These circles of peace fly under the radar of the media and their cities, but their deep connections and spiritual power leaven the movement and the city.

Peacemaking communities are an essential part of the global spread of creative nonviolence. If we pursue the nonviolent life, we may want to join or form such a local peace community. If we dare get beyond our individualistic selves and small words, and reach out to local people who share our struggle, we may find that life becomes fuller—and the work of peace can spread.

9

Driving While Nonviolent

There are many sides to nonviolence. We're just beginning to plumb the mystery, the possibilities, the hope of becoming a nonviolent people. One straightforward, practical measure of our nonviolence is how we drive.

Surely, in the closing days of fossil fuels, the ideal is not to drive at all. Meantime, until cars fall into obsolescence, in this day of road rage and texting and talking on the cell phone, the principles of nonviolence would have us be even more centered and aware, as we drive, so as not to hurt a soul.

That means, of course, no offensive driving and no handheld devices. Rather we embrace good, old-fashioned courtesies. We go the speed limit; we offer a nod to let cars in ahead of us. Without citing the word "nonviolent," *Road and Travel* magazine offers a nice litany of tips for nonviolent driving: don't tailgate, don't cut others off, be magnanimous, offer leeway, don't express anger, don't get drawn into a confrontation.

Of course, these days, it's easier said than done. I violated several of these recently while driving in Honolulu. A side street beckoned, a shortcut to the main road. Thirty miles per hour read the sign on the post. I turned in, only to find myself behind a driver crawling along like a farmer flogging a lazy mule over a hill. In fits and starts we moved ahead, sometimes as slowly as five miles per hour.

I was flooded with annoyance. Why won't she go faster? I thought. My frustration level rose. Is she lost? What possible reason is there for this? Soon we came to an intersection. Inwardly I pleaded with her: "turn right, turn left, go anywhere but straight."

At the intersection she stopped, and stayed stopped long beyond a reasonable hiatus. Then finally, off she crawled—to my disappointment, straight ahead—with the rapidity of a tortoise. Alas, she would be my pacesetter for another block.

By now, I had had enough. I pressed on the horn and blasted the air, a blast good and long. That ought to get her moving, I thought.

Her car lurched to a stop. Out came the driver, apoplectic, a young woman with fury in her eyes. She stormed over to my car window, eyes popping out of her head, and screamed. "What are you doing? Why are you in such a hurry? You're scaring me!" On the instant, I realized my impatience and fell into a case of sheepishness. "I'm so sorry. You're right." Back to her car she stomped, twice looking back with a fierce glare.

As we again crawled ahead, I wondered: what had happened? It was only later that it dawned on me. My boorish behavior had little to do with her or her driving. Rather it had to do with an old pain. That morning, a priest friend I had visited casually uttered the name of a certain church official, one who had written me the year before, urging me to stop my anti-war work (a fairly regular occurrence for me; not a day or a week goes by without this kind of criticism). I thought I had let go and moved on. But here it was again, the wound reopened and there was another spasm of anger and resentment—which I unleashed on the poor driver ahead.

Such is the mechanics of road rage. Some hurt or bitterness stirs anger within us, and along the highway we take it out others. We cut them off, lean on the horn, and fling in their direction a choice and unflattering name. And in the process we put each other in harm's way.

There is a story by a German member of the Order of InterBeing, Thich Nhat Hanh's community. His name is Karl, and he spent a lot of time on the road with Nhat Hanh. Once, on the way to a retreat in Austria, Karl started picking up speed while he was driving. Along he went with gusto, far above the speed limit, the great Thich Nhat Hanh sitting beside him. Soon Nhat Hanh put his hand gently on his arm and said, "Please, Karl, it seems you are driving very fast now." Embarassed, Karl slowed down and kept to the speed limit.

Later, during a rest stop, Nhat Hanh vanished into the woods for a little "walking meditation," and then returned. "I have a gift for you," he told Karl. It was a pine cone. Put it on your dashboard, he said. "Every time you drive faster than the speed limit, it should remind you of my wish that you mindfully take your foot off the gas pedal."

I've taken the story to heart myself. While hiking alone in the Rocky Mountains National Park in Colorado recently, I found a beautiful pine cone and placed it in a conspicuous spot in my truck. It reminds me to drive more nonviolently, more slowly, more peacefully. Sitting there, it also makes me smile; it calls to memory Nhat Hanh's gentle and wise way of teaching us how to be more mindful.

Life is short. I don't want to spend it hurting others; I don't want to hurt anyone ever again. Neither do I want to waste it in useless anger, impatience, or frustration. Nowadays I'm adding to my spiritual disciplines the practice of peaceful driving. As I move along, I listen to music, say my prayers, and enjoy life. I try to avoid the rush and impatience.

Nonviolence is ever unfolding, ever new, ever challenging. It requires vigilance, creativity, helpful reminders and constant reflection about each aspect of our lives. It's a journey, but even so, a nonviolent journey. The deeper we go into the mystery and mysticism of Christian nonviolence, the more we realize, there's no rush. We've already arrived. As Nhat Hanh would say, we're already home.

10

Nonviolence Towards Creation
and All Creatures

Nonviolence is the law of the universe. It's the nature of the Creator and the framework and heart of reality that is still unfolding. So as we try to be nonviolent to ourselves and everyone we meet, we also strive to be nonviolent to creation itself and to all creatures on earth. Nonviolence encompasses our attitude toward everything in the universe. It's the way of enlightenment. It needs to be extended far and wide. As far as the stars!

This means that the days of violence toward the earth and her beautiful creatures are over. Catastrophic climate change has forced all of us to recognize that if we keep on doing violence to creation, we will destroy ourselves in the process. We need to wake up to the ancient wisdom that calls us to honor the earth and all her creatures. We should listen to the indigenous peoples of the world who have told us for centuries that the earth is our mother, and that all creatures are to be reverenced.

"The earth does not belong to us," Chief Seattle once wrote. "We belong to the earth." That wisdom hit me recently as I looked out over the spectacular, wild desert landscape of Southern Utah.

Earlier, I was in Salt Lake City to visit a small peace community that has been meeting every Tuesday afternoon for over ten years. They read peace literature aloud, share personal reflections, and pray together. The group has enriched everyone's life, and deepened their individual faith and sense of peace. After experiencing this beautiful community, I drove down to Moab to Arches National Park and Canyonlands National Park.

Those majestic desert vistas and massive orange rock formations reveal Mother Earth at her most astonishing. The endless vistas, orange cliffs, red boulders and canyons—the fruit of 300 million years of erosion—seem to bear the fingerprints of the Creator. They provide an up close encounter with the Great Mystery. If we listen closely, they teach an ancient wisdom—the way of peace.

Some 2,300 natural rock arches are spread throughout the monumental rock formations, cliffs, boulders and mountains of Arches National Park. Nothing can prepare you for these strange, inspiring orange and red rocks and arches set against the blue sky. At the entrance, you drive high up into the mountains along the sheer orange cliffs and arrive first at "Park Avenue," a narrow valley of sagebrush, low pine trees, cactus, and dead wood lying between ten story brown and orange cliffs and rocks. It feels like you're walking between New York's skyscrapers except that these formations are infinitely more beautiful. Then you drive on to Windows, Delicate Arch, and eventually Devil's Garden, with its bizarre red and orange cliffs sticking up like fins out of the earth. In the distance, a hundred miles of desert spreads out around you, and massive mountains rise on the horizon—the distant Rockies.

I found myself reduced to silence. Just like standing before the Grand Canyon or the ocean or looking up at the night sky and seeing a million stars and the Milky Way in the night sky. I was suddenly very small and quite insignificant in the grand scheme of things. Mother Earth can be humbling.

I couldn't help but think of the Creator. There, before that vista, I entered the spirit of peace and quiet, and learned to breathe and be present all over again. The harsh but beautiful landscape is re-centering. It helps reclaim one's soul and makes one feel more human.

Arches National Park is one of the most spectacular places on earth, but it is just a prelude to Canyonlands, where I also spent many hours driving around, looking at the vistas, and meditating on creation. Canyonlands National Park is Utah's version of the Grand Canyon. It's more accessible than Arizona's Grand

Canyon, since the Colorado and Green Rivers form three sections of Canyonlands, with "Island in the Sky" in the middle, a high plateau in the center of it with views in every direction.

As far as the eye can see are red, orange, brown, and purple cliffs and canyons and rocks and pillars and white salt edges with green pines and sagebrush sprinkled over the landscape. I felt like I'd landed on Mars. Nothing moves. It's like a living painting.

It's so overwhelming that part of you wants to look away and get back to your ordinary day to day business. It's too powerful, too real, too much for the eyes and mind and heart. You can't take it all in.

I wonder if that's why so few spend time with God. Like the universe, God is simply too big, too true, too good, too mysterious, too old, too loving, too overwhelming. Only a few saints and mystics can stand before the reality of God. Only a few dare not run away from the truth of God. Only a few seem to open their hearts to the mystery of God. I certainly don't claim to be one of those few, but I would like to become one, and I know that eventually, like every other human being, I will stand before God. Canyonlands, like the best of Mother Earth, is a good place to practice being humbled before God. We stand still, open ourselves to the universe, awaken to reality, and patiently wait in peace.

There were hardly any tourists that afternoon when I arrived at the Grand View Lookout, so I was able to drink in the silence, open my eyes to the vista before me, listen with my ears, practice mindfulness, enter contemplative peace and be fully present before the revelation.

As I tried to take it in, I noticed that everything was broken— the rocks, cliffs, pillars, boulders and pinnacles. It was the brokenness, caused by time's erosion, that brought about the beauty. There's a lesson there somewhere, I thought.

I've been trying in recent years to spend more quality time with nature—at the ocean, in the desert, by rivers and mountains and woods and fields—and with her creatures, to become one with the earth and find God in God's creation and creatures. This is part of the nonviolent life, too. I want to feel grounded, connected to the earth, especially now as climate change is hitting us. I want to grieve for what we have done to creation and her creatures, and try to side with Mother Earth, that my fledgling nonviolence should somehow extend even to creation and her creatures.

Isn't that what the nonviolent Jesus urged? "Consider the lilies of the field..." "Learn a lesson from the fig tree..." "Look at the birds in the sky..." He wanted us to learn the way of God as he did—from creation and her creatures.

"Blessed are the meek," Jesus teaches in the Beatitudes, "they shall inherit the earth." Right there, at the beginning of the Sermon on the Mount, he connects the life of nonviolence with our oneness with creation. If we can practice biblical meekness—creative nonviolence—we will become one with creation. We will be grounded on earth, respect creation and her creations, and find ourselves at home. We know who we are—sons and daughters of the God of peace.

It's precisely our disconnect from creation that led to the destructive policies that now bring catastrophic climate change. We are not grounded, so we do not inherit the earth. We go through life causing havoc at every level, and know nothing of the beauty or the wisdom of creation. So we don't think twice about destroying the world. Once again, it's because we do not know who we are.

St. Francis of Assisi made the sacred connection between nonviolence and creation. He prayed, served the poor, practiced nonviolence, and walked around saying, "Pace e bene!" ("Peace and goodness!") to all he met. But he also learned the names of the trees, the birds and the flowers, and slept outdoors most of his life. Eventually, as his own people rejected him because of his nonviolence, he ended up alone in a cave. He became one with creation and her creatures. His nonviolence led him to "inherit the earth." He models the life of nonviolence that extends to all creation and her creatures.

Gandhi, too, made this critical connection. Like Francis, he slept outdoors for the last few decades of his life. He knew that creation could sustain humanity, that all the world's poor could get by if we shared equally, justly, what she had to offer. He also suggested that the measure of any civilization is how it treats its animals. He respected the earth and its creatures, insisted that we become vegetarians, and taught a universal nonviolence that would welcome heaven on earth. His vision has yet to be matched. He points the way forward for a comprehensive, holistic life of nonviolence.

Now, on the brink, we need to wake up to the truth of reality—that we are all one, that we are physically united to creation and her creatures, that we need to be nonviolent toward the earth itself, and the air and water and all creatures—if we want to survive and live in peace.

Many scientific reports claim that if we do not radically change our global policies and practices, a frightening apocalypse of violence will bear down upon us. As the population rises to ten billion by the end of the century, there will likely be over a hundred wars over water, with rampant starvation, disease and extreme poverty, killing millions, perhaps billions of sisters and brothers. Within a few hundred years, only half the planet will be inhabitable, and the global population may fall as low as 250 million people.

"Whatever befalls the earth, befalls the sons and daughters of the earth," Chief Seattle wrote long ago. He was right. We need to heed his wisdom and change our lives.

So from now on, we need to take action to protect creation and her creatures, to stop every act of violence and destruction of the environment. We can live more simply, use alternative sources of energy like wind and solar power, be nonviolent to all animals, and change the way we eat, what we wear, how often we drive and fly, what we buy and where we live. We can explore our local surroundings, eat organically, become vegetarians, pitch in with volunteer groups to clean up and protect creation, and study its beauty. More, we can join the movements that resist the destruction of the earth—from fracking and the use of oil to the big business of animal slaughterhouses to war and nuclear weapons which destroy creation. As we join the struggle to side with Mother Earth and change destructive systems with pro-earth policies, we join with the universe itself and find the God of peace all around us.

Where do we begin? Environmental groups offer many concrete steps. For example, www.50waystohelp.com lists a variety of simple actions: change your light bulbs; turn off your computers at night; recycle everything; don't rinse your dishes or preheat your oven; wash in cold or warm; hang dry your clothes; don't use paper napkins; use both sides of paper; recycle paper; don't take baths; don't use plastic bags; don't use any plastic bottles; take shorter showers; drive less; bicycle more; turn off your lights; don't use any plastic; use less heat or air conditioning; buy local; plant a tree; and so forth.

Environmentalist Sarah van Gelder suggests three basic steps as we grapple with the depressing reality of catastrophic climate change:

> *First, let reality sink in.* This is not the future we thought we would have. Young people especially have the right to be disappointed, angry, and fearful. It will take courage to face this new normal, especially when so many others remain disconnected from what's happening. By being mindful of your own emotions, you can experience fear or grief without being overwhelmed by those feelings. And by remaining alert to the way the climate crisis may show up in your life, you can be better prepared and more resilient...

Second, take a stand. We may be too late to stop the climate from shifting, but we can likely stop the most catastrophic effects of climate change. People of all ages are stepping up to block extraction, transportation, and burning of fossil fuels and to challenge the clout of the fossil fuel lobby. Some are doing it to protect their community's water or air or their own health; others are motivated by concern for climate stability and the lives of generations to come...

Third, consider ways to replace the consumer-oriented, energy-intensive ways of life that are unaffordable both for many of our families and for the planet. Young people especially are finding satisfaction in what they contribute, the depth of friendships, and in personal development – rather than in "having stuff." Building relationships founded in trust and reciprocity increases our quality of life and resilience, and builds the foundation for the life-centered – rather than consumption-centered – world that can thrive within the constraints of a small planet.

The news about the climate is daunting, but we don't have to wait for skeptics or politicians to get it. We can act right now by getting real about what's happening, taking a stand to stop further damage to our climate, and working together to build a world that treasures the precious diversity of life on this planet – including human life today and in the future. [*Climate Change Is Happening But We Can Meet the Challenge,* June 7, 2013, www.commondreams.org]

I thought of this as I stood before the majestic Canyonlands of Utah, and tried taking it in—the beauty of the gorgeous desert landscapes, and the violence we do to it all: fracking, drilling for oil, poisoning the water and the land, building and using nuclear weapons, ignoring the starving millions, dropping bombs and maintaining a culture of permanent war. Can we choose to protect creation, reverse our destructive policies and save ourselves? The God of peace hopes we will.

As we consciously try to practice nonviolence toward the earth, we also try to be meticulously nonviolent to all her creatures: dogs, cats, horses, cows, chickens, sheep, birds, pelicans, hawks, eagles, fish, whales, deer, buffalo, coyote, wolves, snakes, insects, giraffes, elephants, rhinoceros, lions, tigers and the rest. The abuse, violence and killing of animals around the planet is unconscionable, beyond imagining and taken for granted. In the U.S., animal cruelty is rampant. Around the world, violence towards creatures is perfectly normal.

We need to rethink our relationship to the amazing creatures that God has placed among us. We can stop killing them, stop eating them, and start caring for them. We can join PETA (People for the Ethical Treatment of Animals), and our local humane society. They will help us grow in awareness, strengthen our universal nonviolence and help us educate others about nonviolence toward the earth's creatures.

Like creation itself, animals teach us about ourselves. They show us how to be human. If we dare extend our nonviolence to them, they will point us to the Creator, to the source of life, to the wisdom of peace. Dogs and cats show us love and affection, horses inspire us with their intelligence, and the great creatures— tigers, whales, elephants—astonish us with their majesty. Why would we harm them, or kill them? For money? Even in all their wildness, they teach us new depths of nonviolence. Animals, too, are sacred for they have the life of God within them.

At the end of my day at Canyonlands, at the Visitors' Center, I asked one of the Rangers, an elderly Minnesotan woman with white hair and a big smile, what it all means. "I'm speechless before these canyons," I confessed.

"You're on the right track," she said with a smile, pointing to my heart. "These canyons, rocks, cliffs and rivers touch us at a very deep level. They connect to our soul. The challenge is to stay with them and listen to them."

For centuries these sacred lands have held a silent peace witness before us. When I put my ear to the ground, I hear a prayer that we might reclaim our true nonviolent nature, our "meekness," and do what we can to protect creation and her creatures, that we might save the earth and future generations from our senseless violence. It's a worthy struggle. One that offers the blessing of Jesus himself—and the earth as our personal inheritance.

As we grow in awareness and reverence toward all of creation and her creatures and take action to save the planet and all life, we will discover new depths of nonviolence, and help give birth to universal nonviolence.

Questions for Personal Reflection and Small Group Discussion

How can we become more nonviolent to those we know and meet? Where do we need to improve our nonviolence—among our families, friends, workplace, church, peace groups? How can we practice a meticulous interpersonal nonviolence?

Who challenges our nonviolence most? How do we practice nonviolence to those who are violent toward us? Where do we find the God of peace as we practice interpersonal nonviolence?

How can small, ordinary, day-to-day encounters help us strengthen our nonviolence so that we will be better able to practice nonviolence in our public work, demonstrations, and movements? In what areas of life, such as our driving, can we become more nonviolent?

How can we create more inclusive circles of peace and nonviolence in our lives? How can we help our local communities become communities of nonviolence? How can we start a new community of peace and nonviolence around us?

How do we support catastrophic violence toward the environment and her creatures? Where do we need to change our habits and living situations so that we do no harm to creation and her creatures? How can we be more nonviolent to animals and all creatures? What can we do to protect and sustain creation and her creatures? How can we deepen our respect and reverence for creation and her creatures? Where do we find the God of peace in creation and among her creatures?

97

Part Three

Joining the Global Grassroots Movement of Nonviolence

We have to make truth and nonviolence not matters for mere individual practice but for practice by groups and communities and nations. That at any rate is my dream. I shall live and die in trying to realize it.
— Gandhi

An individual has not started living until he (or she) can rise above the narrow confines of his (or her) individualistic concerns to the broader concerns of all humanity.
— Martin Luther King, Jr.

One is called to live nonviolently, even if the social or political change one worked for is in fact unlikely or even impossible.
— Daniel Berrigan

It is time for people to rise to their full moral and spiritual height, to take the world on their shoulders, and to say, "I will save the earth."
— Dr. Helen Caldicott

We can change the world if we do it nonviolently. If we can just show people how they can organize nonviolently, we can't fail. Nonviolence has never failed when it's been tried.
— Cesar Chavez

11

There *Is* a Global Grassroots Movement of Nonviolence, And It's Changing the World for the Better

"Nonviolence is fine as long as it works," Malcolm X once said. Deep down, he probably thought, like most of us, that it doesn't work. You'd never know from watching FOX News that organized nonviolent resistance on a national level could bring dramatic nonviolent change, or that a global grassroots movement of nonviolence was slowly sweeping over the world. You don't read about it much in the *New York Times* or *The Washington Post*. The mainstream U.S. media is not interested in nonviolent social change. They're trying to make billions of dollars, and that's not what nonviolence is about.

Wars, weapons, poverty and destructive environmental policies threaten us all. At the same time though, people are on the move, activating nonviolent change. All around the world they are waking up, meeting, organizing, demonstrating, speaking out and challenging the culture of violence and injustice, armed only with the power of nonviolence. And they are making a positive, and lasting, difference.

Because of the global nonviolence movement, this is one of the most exciting times in history to be alive. Finally, we are being forced to wake up to what our global violence is doing to us—and to what organized nonviolence has the potential to do for us.

"The choice is no longer violence or nonviolence," Dr. King said in Memphis the night before he was shot dead. "It's nonviolence or non-existence." How right he was! If we do not become people of nonviolence and join this global movement, we will destroy ourselves. We have to choose nonviolence for ourselves individually, nationally and globally. Even though the U.S. government's military outreach and destructive policies, along with the other world powers, seem invincible, the grassroots movement continues to spread across the globe in pursuit of nonviolent change for justice and peace. Since change only comes from the bottom up, those movements hold great promise—but only if every one of us gets involved.

Nonviolence would never work against the Nazis, most people say. But that's not true. Where organized nonviolent resistance was tried, it worked—in Denmark, Norway and Bulgaria, and in pockets throughout Europe. Nonviolent resistance to the Nazis needs to be studied more closely and taught more widely. Nonviolence quite likely would have been used more widely in resisting the Nazis had people across Europe been trained in the discipline and power of nonviolent change—and had they developed the infrastructure for society-wide nonviolent resistance before or during the emergence of the Third Reich. In the cases where it was deployed, it was often improvised. Given the successes in places like Denmark, one can imagine that systematic, wholesale nonviolent non-cooperation with the evil policies of the Nazis—a great risk though such resistance would be—could have challenged Germany's project. Of course, this would have taken immense courage, training, and organization, as well as a canny ability to read the signs of the times, in order to have mounted widespread nonviolent opposition in the early stages of the Third Reich to deny it the pillars of social, cultural, political and economic support on which it depended.

We have seen how violent resistance to the Nazis led many people—Soviets and Americans alike—to become like Nazis, to the point of vaporizing hundreds of thousands of people in Japan with nuclear weapons, and embarking on fifty years of Cold War insanity that threatened human itself. We need to learn the power of organized nonviolent national resistance to insane militaristic nations. We need to begin the long journey of disarming the nations—beginning with the world's greatest superpower, the United States—and then strengthening the United Nations to coordinate international nonviolent conflict resolution and new nonviolent civilian based defense systems. All of this is possible, if we have the political will and spiritual commitment to make it come true.

In the midst of the twentieth century's worst horrors, the best organized movements of nonviolence in history unfolded—starting with Gandhi's nonviolent independence campaign against British imperialism, and Dr. King's nonviolent Civil Rights movement against racist American segregation. What we forget is that these movements led to thousands of other nonviolent movements that are still unfolding today. The anti-Vietnam movement, the women's movement, the environmental movement, the gay and lesbian movement, the anti-death penalty movement, the anti-nuclear movement, and countless others owe a profound debt to the vision and strategic action of Gandhi and King. Within decades, the Marcos dictatorship was brought down; the Soviet Union collapsed; apartheid was abolished; Nelson Mandela became president of South Africa; Liberian women nonviolently overthrew the deadly dictatorship of Charles Taylor; the Occupy movement fought Wall Street greed; the Arab Spring began to wake up those living under Middle Eastern dictatorship; and millions marched against poverty in Brazil. And these are only the most well known examples. Over 900 other cases are documented and analyzed on the Global Nonviolent Action Database, see: www.nvdatabase.swarthmore.edu.

On February 12, 2003, some twelve million people marched in over 620 cities on every continent in protest of a war that hadn't even begun yet. It was the single greatest day of protest in the history of the world. This alone was an incredible historical breakthrough that still promises to bear good fruit for humanity. The U.S. attack on Iraq was not prevented, but the peace movement continued to grow and eventually created the political conditions to bring the war to an end. As the *New York Times* said in an editorial the next day after the global mobilization, the world now has two superpowers—the United States and the global grassroots peace movement.

When we use our political power for positive change, we discover we are stronger than we once thought. That grassroots peace movement needs every one of us if it is to blossom and bring forth a full harvest. It needs our full-time commitment, our lifelong persistent participation, especially given the gravity of our global predicament.

"We can change the world if we do it nonviolently," Cesar Chavez once said. "If we can just show people how they can organize nonviolently, we can't fail. Nonviolence has never failed when it's been tried."

In recent decades, as Walter Wink and others have pointed out, some two thirds of the human race has been personally involved in local, national, or international struggles for justice and peace. That's an astonishing fact, one you won't hear on the nightly news. People *are* moving. They are getting involved to change the unjust status quo. And they're using the only weapon available to them—the power of nonviolence. What's even more astonishing than the massive numbers involved in this emerging global struggle is the evidence that when active, organized nonviolence is applied to entrenched violent establishments, it works!

Unlike violence, organized nonviolent movements often fly under the pro-war media radar. They're slow, and rarely televised. While violence makes the evening news—with daily terrorist bombings, drone attacks, corporate greed and military lies— nonviolence remains hard to measure, hard to quantify, and sometimes hard to see. Yet it builds up and grows slowly until, suddenly, it appears like a tidal wave out of nowhere—like the People Power movement which swept the Filipino Marcos dictatorship out in four days. Suddenly, peaceful revolution occurs and the streets are filled with celebration. No one ever asks how it happened. Usually, it was preceded by years, even decades, of quiet movement building, organizing and nonviolence training.

The media prefer to cover the bloodshed of war. Peace is boring, they say. What they don't know is that peace is our only hope, and is not one bit boring. They would discover this if they dared to give our provocative peacemaking thinkers significant air time. Peacemakers are often quite charismatic, and peace movements are often thrilling to watch unfold. It's amazing to witness ordinary people who join the cause, become empowered, and take action for justice and peace. That's the story of ordinary people like Rosa Parks, Fannie Lou Hamer, John Lewis, and Bayard Rustin who became legendary Civil Rights heroes. It's the story of everyone who gets involved in the global grassroots movement of nonviolence.

Nonviolent Resistance Works

Recently, Columbia University Press published an extraordinary scholarly book that proves how nonviolence works far better as a method for social change than violence. This breakthrough work demonstrates that Gandhi was right all along, that the method of nonviolent resistance as a way to social change usually leads to a more lasting peace, while violence usually fails. It challenges all of us to teach this methodology of global change, and more, to join the struggle.

Why Civil Resistance Works: The Strategic Logic of Nonviolent Conflict by Erica Chenoweth and Maria J. Stephan uses graphs, charts, sociological research and statistical analysis to show how over the last century nonviolent movements were far better at mobilizing supporters, resisting regime crackdowns, creating new initiatives, defeating repressive regimes and establishing lasting democracies. Their evidence points to the conclusion that nonviolent resistance works far better than armed resistance in overturning oppressive and repressive regimes, and in leading to more democratic societies.

This report should cause the whole world to take up nonviolent conflict resolution and nonviolent resistance to injustice, instead of maintaining the tired, obsolete methods of war and violence.

Why Civil Resistance Works is the first systematic study of its kind, and takes us beyond the brilliant research of Gene Sharp and other pioneering analysts of nonviolent power to demonstrate once and for all the power of nonviolent civil resistance for positive social change. One wishes the U.S. government would learn its lessons, renounce its violence and start supporting nonviolent, people power movements. But if the government refuses the wisdom of nonviolence, we the people need not be so naïve or ignorant. We need to do our homework, and learn what's worked in past struggles as we embark on even greater struggles.

For more than a century, from 1900 to 2006, campaigns of nonviolent resistance were "more than twice as effective as their violent counterparts in achieving their stated goals," the authors conclude. By attracting widespread popular support through protests, boycotts, civil disobedience and other forms of nonviolent noncooperation, these campaigns broke repressive regimes and brought major new changes for justice and peace. Much of the book focuses on four case studies to explain their conclusions—the Iranian revolution of 1977-1979; the first Palestinian Intifada of 1987-1992; the Filipino People Power revolution of 1983-1986; and the Burmese uprising of 1988-1990.

Through their statistical analysis, they found that nonviolent resistance presents "fewer obstacles to moral and physical involvement and commitment, and that higher levels of participation contribute to enhanced resilience, greater opportunities for tactical innovation and civic disruption (and therefore less incentive for a regime to maintain its status quo), and shifts in loyalty among opponents' supporters, including members of the military establishment."

106

Contrary to popular belief, "violent insurgency is rarely justifiable on strategic grounds," they write. "Nonviolent resistance ushers in more durable and internally peaceful democracies, which are less likely to regress into civil war."

"We analyzed 323 violent and nonviolent resistance campaigns between 1900 and 2006," the authors explain in their introduction.

> Among them are over one hundred major nonviolent campaigns since 1900, whose frequency has increased over time. In addition to their growing frequency, the success rates of nonviolent campaigns have increased. How does this compare with violent insurgencies? One might assume that the success rates may have increased among both nonviolent and violent insurgencies. But in our data, we find the opposite: although they persist, the success rates of violent insurgencies have declined. The most striking finding is that between 1900 and 2006, nonviolent resistance campaigns were nearly twice as likely to achieve full or partial success as their violent counterparts. Among the 323 campaigns in the case of anti-regime resistance campaigns, the use of a nonviolent strategy has greatly enhanced the likelihood of success... This book investigates the reasons why—in spite of conventional wisdom to the contrary—civil resistance campaigns have been so effective compared with their violent counterparts.

While 26% of violent campaigns succeed, 54% of nonviolent campaigns succeed, they report. "Nonviolent resistance campaigns are twice as effective as violent ones in achieving their goals...We argue that nonviolent campaigns fail to achieve their objectives when they are unable to overcome the challenge of participation, when they fail to recruit a robust, diverse, and broad-based membership that can erode the power base of the adversary and maintain resilience in the face of repression." That's why we all need to get involved: to help nonviolent campaigns reach their objections.

The evidence of their research points to the superiority of nonviolent resistance at every level, including against genocidal regimes. "The claim that nonviolent resistance could never work against genocidal foes like Adolph Hitler and Joseph Stalin is the classic straw man put forward to demonstrate the inherent limitations of this form of struggle," they note.

> While it is possible that nonviolent resistance could not be used effectively once genocide has broken out in full force, this claim is not backed by any strong empirical evidence. Collective nonviolent struggle was not used with any strategic forethought during World War II, nor was it ever contemplated as an overall strategy for resisting the Nazis. Violent resistance, which some groups attempted for ending Nazi occupation, was also an abject failure. However, scholars have found that certain forms of collective nonviolent resistance were, in fact, occasionally successful in resisting Hitler's occupation policies. The case of the Danish population's resistance to German occupation is an example of partially effective civil resistance in an extremely difficult environment.

> The famous case of the Rosenstrasse protests, when German women of Aryan descent stood for a week outside a detention center on the Rosenstrasse in Berlin demanding the release of their Jewish husbands, who were on the verge of being deported to concentration camps, is a further example of limited gains against a genocidal regime brought about by civil resistance. The German women, whose numbers increased as the protests continued and they attracted more attention, were sufficiently disruptive with their sustained nonviolent protests that the Nazi officials eventually released their Jewish husbands...The notion that nonviolent action can be successful only if the adversary does not use violent repression is neither theoretically nor historically substantiated.

These studies "call for scholars to rethink power and its sources in any given society or polity," the authors suggest. "Our findings demonstrate that power actually depends on the consent of the civilian population, consent that can be withdrawn and reassigned to more legitimate or more compelling parties... We hope that this book challenges the conventional wisdom concerning the effectiveness of nonviolent struggle and encourages scholars and policy makers to take seriously the role that civilians play in actively prosecuting conflict without resorting to violence."

I have long believed that Gandhi—and Jesus—were right to insist on the method of nonviolent resistance, for both moral and practical reasons, but now the facts are in. The evidence is all laid out in this scholarly report.

"Nonviolent resistance can be a near-unstoppable force for change in our world, even in the most unlikely circumstances," these scholars conclude. Their research proves Gandhi's insight that mobilized nonviolent resistance is the best weapon for peaceful change. The only catch with mobilized, global nonviolent movements for social change is that they require everyone's participation. Each one of us has to get personally involved in the global grassroots movement of nonviolence.

That means you and me—and all of us.

12

Dr. King's "To Do" List

After Rosa Parks refused to take a seat at the back of the bus, broke the segregation law, and was arrested on December 1, 1955, the African-American leadership in Montgomery famously chose young Rev. Dr. Martin Luther King, Jr. to lead their campaign. He was an unknown quantity. Certainly no one expected him to emerge as a Moses-like tower of strength. No one imagined that he would invoke Gandhi's method of nonviolent resistance in Christian language as the basis for the boycott. But from day one, he was a force to be reckoned with.

With the help of Bayard Rustin and Glenn Smiley of the Fellowship of Reconciliation, Dr. King articulated a methodology of nonviolence that still rings true. It's an ethic of nonviolent resistance that's also a strategy of hope, which can help us today in the thousands of Montgomery-like movements around the world, including the Occupy movements and the ongoing Arab Spring movements.

Dr. King outlined his way of nonviolence in his 1958 account of the Montgomery movement, *Stride Toward Freedom* (Harper and Row, pp. 83-88). There he tells the story of the movement and his own personal journey, then offers six, basic points for nonviolence. Dr. King lived and taught these essential ingredients of active nonviolence until the day he died. (For an excellent commentary on them, I recommend *Roots of Resistance: The Nonviolent Ethic of Martin Luther King, Jr.*, by William D. Watley, Valley Forge, Judson Press, 1985.)

These fundamental principles, along with his six steps for nonviolent action, make up Dr. King's "to do" list:

First, nonviolence is the way of the strong. Nonviolence is not for the cowardly, the weak, the passive, the apathetic, or the fearful. "Nonviolent resistance does resist," he wrote. "It is not a method of stagnant passivity. While the nonviolent resister is passive in the sense that he is not physically aggressive toward his opponent, his mind and emotions are always active, constantly seeking to persuade his opponent that he is wrong. The method is passive physically, but strongly active spiritually. It is not passive non-resistance to evil; it is active nonviolent resistance to evil."

Second, the goal of nonviolence is redemption and reconciliation. "Nonviolence does not seek to defeat or humiliate the opponent but to win friendship and understanding," King teaches. "The nonviolent resister must often express his protest through noncooperation or boycotts, but he realizes that these are not ends themselves; they are merely means to awaken a sense of moral shame in the opponent... The aftermath of nonviolence is the creation of the beloved community, while the aftermath of violence is tragic bitterness."

Third, nonviolence seeks to defeat evil, not people. Nonviolence is directed "against forces of evil rather than against persons who happen to be doing the evil. It is evil that the nonviolent resister seeks to defeat, not the persons victimized by evil."

"Not only did King depersonalize the goal of nonviolence by defining it in terms of reconciliation rather than the defeat of the opponent, but he also depersonalized the target of the nonviolent resister's attack," Watley writes. "The opponent for King is a symbol of a greater evil... The evildoers were victims of evil as much as were the individuals and communities that the evildoers oppressed." In this thinking, King echoes St. Paul's admonition that our struggle is ultimately not against particular people but systems—"the principalities and powers."

Fourth, nonviolence includes a willingness to accept suffering without retaliation, to accept blows from the opponent without striking back. "The nonviolent resister is willing to accept violence if necessary, but never to inflict it," King writes. "Unearned suffering is redemptive. Suffering, the nonviolent resister realizes, has tremendous educational and transforming possibilities." That's a tough pill to swallow but King insists that there is power in the acceptance of unearned suffering love, as the nonviolent resister Jesus showed on Calvary and Dr. King himself showed in his own life and death.

In *Stride Toward Freedom*, King urged nonviolent resisters to paraphrase Gandhi and say: "We will match your capacity to inflict suffering with our capacity to endure suffering. We will meet your physical force with soul force. We will not hate you, but we cannot in all good conscience obey your unjust laws. Do to us what you will and we will still love you. Bomb our homes and threaten our children; send your hooded perpetrators of violence into our communicates and drag us out on some wayside road, beating us and leaving us half dead, and we will still love you. But we will soon wear you down by our capacity to suffer. And in winning our freedom we will so appeal to your heart and conscience that we will win you in the process." (p. 194)

Fifth, nonviolence avoids not only external physical violence but also internal violence of spirit. It practices agape/love in action. "The nonviolent resister not only refuses to shoot his opponent; he also refuses to hate him. At the center of nonviolence stands the principle of love." Cutting off the chain of hate "can only be done by projecting the ethic of love to the center of our lives." Love means "understanding, redemptive good will toward all people." For King, this agape/love is the power of God working within us, Watley explains. That is why King could exhort us to the highest possible, unconditional, universal, all-encompassing love. King the preacher believed that God worked through us when we used the weapon of nonviolent love.

Sixth, nonviolence is based on the conviction that the universe is on the side of justice. "The believer in nonviolence has deep faith in the future," King writes. "He knows that in his struggle for justice he has cosmic companionship. There is a creative force in this universe that works to bring the disconnected aspects of reality into a harmonious whole." King's philosophy, spirituality, theology and methodology were rooted in hope.

These core principles explain why, as King used to say, nonviolence was "the morally excellent way." As he boldly expanded his campaign from Montgomery to Atlanta, Albany and eventually Birmingham, he demonstrated six basic steps of nonviolent action that could be applied to any nonviolent movement for social change.

The Six Stages of a Nonviolent Campaign

As explained in *Active Nonviolence* (Vol. I, ed. by Richard Deats, The Fellowship of Reconciliation, 1991), every campaign of nonviolence usually undergoes these basic stages toward justice, and they are worth our consideration:

First, information gathering. We need to do our homework, and learn everything we can about the issue, problem or injustice so that we become experts on the topic.

Second, education. Then we do our best to inform everyone, including the opposition, about the issue, and use every form of media to educate the population.

Third, personal commitment. As we engage in the public struggle for nonviolent social change, we renew ourselves every day in the way of nonviolence. As we learn that nonviolent struggles take time, we commit ourselves to the long haul and do the hard inner work necessary to center ourselves in love and wisdom, and prepare ourselves for the possibility of rejection, arrest, jail or suffering for the cause.

Fourth, negotiations. We try to engage our opponent, point out their injustice, propose a way out, and resolve the situation, using win-win strategies.

Fifth, direct action. If necessary, we take nonviolent direct action to force the opponent to deal with the issue and resolve the injustice, using nonviolent means such as boycotts, marches, rallies, petitions, voting campaigns and civil disobedience.

Sixth, reconciliation. In the end, we try to reconcile with our opponents, even to become their friends (as Nelson Mandela demonstrated in South Africa), so that we all can begin to heal and move closer to the vision of the "beloved community."

Dr. King's principles and methodology of nonviolence outline a path to social change that still holds true. In his strategy, the ends are already present in the means; the seeds of a peaceful outcome can be found in our peaceful means. He argues that if we resist injustice through steadfast nonviolence and build a movement along these lines, we take the high ground as demonstrated in the lives of Jesus and Gandhi and can redeem society and create a new culture of nonviolence.

"May all who suffer oppression in this world reject the self-defeating method of retaliatory violence and choose the method that seeks to redeem," Dr. King concluded. "Through using this method wisely and courageously we will emerge from the bleak and desolate midnight of 'man's inhumanity to man' into the bright daybreak of freedom and justice."

Shortly before he died, Dr. King was reflecting on the need and the possibilities of "internationalizing" his nonviolence movement. He didn't live to pursue that vision, so we have to take up where he left off.

"Can a nonviolent, direct-action movement find application on the international level, to confront economic and political problems?" King asked. "I believe it can. It is clear to me that the next stage of the movement is to become international...Although it is obvious that nonviolent movements for social change must internationalize, because of the interlocking nature of the problems we all face, and because otherwise those problems will breed war, we have hardly begun to build the skills and the strategy, or even the commitment, to planetize our movement for social justice... We live each day on the verge of nuclear coannihilation. In this world, nonviolence is no longer an option for intellectual analysis, it is an imperative for action." [*A Testament of Hope*, p. 658.]

An imperative for action! That's the final word of Dr. King. The nonviolent life demands public action as a moral and spiritual imperative.

13

The Birmingham Pledge of Nonviolence

The 1963 Birmingham, Alabama Civil Rights campaign, which led to the March on Washington and historic Civil Rights legislation, shows how Dr. King put these principles into practice and how we can, too. That 1963 David-and-Goliath-like battle pitted Martin Luther King, Jr., school children and the best of the Civil Rights movement against vicious police Chief Eugene "Bull" Connor, the Ku Klux Klan and white racists and demonstrated to the world the power of organized nonviolence.

We remember how high school and elementary school kids marched by the thousands from the 16th Street Baptist church into Kelly Ingram Park and faced down the fire men, German Shepherds, and loaded guns. We remember Dr. King's Good Friday arrest, and the document he produced behind bars, one of the most significant in our history, "Letter from a Birmingham Jail." Combined with the economic boycott of downtown white businesses, these public protests—and the subsequent overcrowded jails, international TV coverage and national outrage—were too much for the white establishment, and segregation fell.

The climactic moment occurred on May 5, 1963, the third day into their "D-Day" children's campaign, when thousands of children marched through the streets right up to the firemen. In the days before, many were brutalized when those fire hoses were turned on them. But the youth learned the lessons of Dr. King. "Nonviolent suffering love is always redemptive," he said in every talk. "We will match your capacity to inflict suffering with our capacity to accept suffering and we will wear you down until justice comes."

So they came back, asking for more. Bull Connor went ballistic. "Turn on the hoses," he screamed at the firemen. The marchers knelt in prayer. "We're not turning back," they said. They stood up and walked right toward the firemen.

"It was one of the most fantastic events of the Birmingham story," King later said. "I saw there, I felt there, for the first time, the pride and power of nonviolence."

While Bull Connor screamed and yelled, the white firemen and police officers were overcome by the singing youth. The firemen couldn't bring themselves to hurt the kids again. So they put down the fire hoses. Some of them started crying. The singing youth walked right through them.

Dr. King and the Birmingham resisters did everything Jesus taught in the Sermon on the Mount. They prove that Jesus' method works. They model the Christian way.

How were those youth able to reach the heights of daring nonviolence? There are many reasons, but first we need to remember that few people in this culture of violence know how to be nonviolent. We're all brainwashed into violence. We have learned well how to be violent. We now have to unlearn those lessons and learn how to be nonviolent. We need to be trained in nonviolence. The Birmingham movement worked hard for many months training everyone, including the youth, in the practice and methodology of nonviolence. Every participant was required to undergo nonviolence training. And they learned their lesson well.

They were also required to sign a pledge of nonviolence, which was written by my friend Rev. James Lawson. That training and signed commitment, within the context of the strong local and national movement, the brilliant organizing, the willingness to risk jail and death, and the charismatic leadership of Dr. King, channeled the energy of the youth into a contagious force of nonviolence that would wear down even the most hardened white racist and our worst apartheid.

With George Wallace, Bull Connor had come to symbolize the worst of the white Southern establishment. He used violence to defend racism, segregation, killings, bombings, systemic injustice, corporate greed and oppression of the poor. King and his associates went to Birmingham deliberately to provoke Connor's extreme wrath to reveal publicly the depths of racist violence and spark a national transformation through the movement's nonviolent suffering love.

Fifty years later, Bull Connor and the white Birmingham establishment have become, to my mind, a symbol of our current government, military and corporate leaders, who defend our unjust structure, corporate greed, banks, gun makers, oil companies, weapons manufacturers, and the one percent, while our drones and bombs kill children around the world, and our nuclear weapons and destructive environmental policies threaten us all. The Bull Connor spirit of violence runs our nation and the world.

Likewise, the thousands of young activists fifty years ago who committed themselves to nonviolence and marched into the face of the fire hoses symbolize the way forward for any who care about the world and its need for justice and disarmament.

If this analogy holds, then Birmingham of 1963 has become the nation, if not the world. We are on one side or the other. We either side with our Bull Connor government and its lethal ways, or with the grassroots movement of nonviolence that continues to grow around the world.

I think we can choose to live in the spirit of those nonviolent youth, resisting our Bull Connor government and its militaristic, violent, unjust ways, and play our part in the global grassroots movement of nonviolence.

One way to do that is to commit ourselves to the Birmingham pledge of nonviolence and try, as Dr. King urged those young marchers, to make active nonviolence a way of life, so that we will be nonviolent but resist state violence in all its forms, and pursue a vision of transformation that seems, for the moment, impossible.

Here's the original pledge:

I hereby pledge myself—my person and body—to the nonviolent movement. Therefore I will keep the following ten commandments:

1. *Meditate daily on the teachings and life of Jesus.*
2. *Remember always that the nonviolent movement seeks justice and reconciliation, not victory.*
3. *Walk and talk in the manner of love, for God is love.*
4. *Pray daily to be used by God in order that all men and women might be free.*
5. *Sacrifice personal wishes in order that all men and women might be free*
6. *Observe with both friend and foe the ordinary rules of courtesy.*
7. *Seek to perform regular service for others and for the world.*
8. *Refrain from the violence of fist, tongue, or heart.*
9. *Strive to be in good spiritual and bodily health.*
10. *Follow the directions of the movement.*

This beautiful pledge of nonviolence offers guide posts for us in our pursuit of the abolition of war, poverty, the death penalty, racism, sexism, corporate greed, catastrophic climate change, and nuclear weapons.

"Meditate. Remember. Walk. Pray. Sacrifice. Observe. Seek. Refrain. Strive. Follow." If we live in that spirit, then we can help build a global movement that can resist our Bull Connor government and transform our Birmingham world.

The 1963 Birmingham campaign teaches us what happens when everyone pitches in and joins the nonviolent movement. I hope more and more of us can find new strength and energy, perhaps through this pledge of nonviolence, to step out publicly and stay involved in the movements for justice and peace.

As Dr. King teaches and Birmingham demonstrates, with active nonviolence—and the God of peace—anything is possible.

14

Get Involved in the Global Movement for Justice, Peace and Creation — and Stay Involved!

"What are you going to do today to fight injustice and global evil?" That's the question the mother of legendary singer and activist Harry Belafonte told him to ask himself every morning when he woke up: "What am I going to do today for peace and justice for humanity?"

In his beautiful memoir, *My Song*, Belafonte tells how he has asked himself that question every morning of his life since he was a little boy. It became his mantra. He has tried to begin every day by determining what practical action he will take that day to help end poverty, war, racism, and systemic evil.

By doing this, Belafonte gave his life focus, purpose and meaning. By staying with that question every day of his life, he has remained committed to the struggle and made a huge difference for all of us.

Every one of us can start our day by asking ourselves that question, Harry Belafonte writes. "What can I do today to promote justice, disarmament, nonviolence and peace? What concrete action can I take to help end violence, war, poverty, racism and evil? How can I practice creative nonviolence, relieve unjust suffering, and help disarm the world? How can I serve God's reign of justice and peace today? How can I help more people become nonviolent? How can I help build the global grassroots movement of nonviolence?" These are good questions to take every morning to God in our quiet meditation.

Mahatma Gandhi and Martin Luther King, Jr. both insisted that nonviolence requires a profound commitment—as well as serious movement organizing. They taught that living and advocating the life of nonviolence, given our global addiction to violence, was the highest human ideal. If we are to survive, all our institutions, structures, and nations will have to become nonviolent, and each one of us is needed to help bring about this global transformation.

Each one of us is going to have to get involved in the global grassroots movements of nonviolence and do what we can to promote justice, disarmament and peace for the human family and all creation, if we are to move forward and create a more nonviolent world. Each one of us has a part to play, a job to do, a role to fill.

My contention is that we have to try to be nonviolent to ourselves and practice nonviolence toward all people we meet and know, but we can't stop there. We have to go farther. If our nonviolence is to serve God's reign of peace, we need to join the growing global grassroots movement of nonviolence for justice and peace, and take some positive public, nonviolent action for humanity and creation. To reach our true potential as sons and daughters of the God of peace, we need to help God as God works to disarm the human race and transform our world.

We can't be just try to be peaceful in our personal lives and do nothing about the world of total violence and permanent war. Nor can we practice attentive nonviolence solely to those around us, and ignore the plight of the suffering masses. We need to make the connections, practice nonviolence at every level, and do our part to help disarm the world. When we join the global grassroots movement of nonviolence, we practice the full, holistic "nonviolence of the strong" taught by Jesus, Gandhi, King, Dorothy Day and many others.

Shortly before he died, I asked the labor organizer and advocate of nonviolence Cesar Chavez what I should tell people when they asked my advice about practicing nonviolence. Without missing a beat, he said, "Tell everyone to engage in public action for peace and justice." He repeated the words over and over again: "Public action, public action, public action! That's the solution!" *Everyone has to engage in public action for peace and justice!*

I've never heard better advice than that.

Shortly before he was assassinated, Archbishop Oscar Romero of El Salvador said, "No one can do everything, but everyone can do something!" This, too, is practical and helpful.

Every one of us is needed in this historic moment to join the global grassroots movement of nonviolence and keep it moving forward if we are to disarm and transform the world. Every one of us has a talent, a gift, to offer. Every one of us has some unique contribution to make to the global movement. The good news is that we don't have to do everything. We only have to do something. But it is incredibly important that each one of us do what we can.

"People equate nonviolence with inaction, with not doing anything," Cesar Chavez wrote, "and it's not that at all. It's exactly the opposite... Nonviolence is action. Like anything else, though, it's got to be organized."

I recommend picking one cause that's close to our hearts and getting involved in that struggle with all our heart and energy. In doing so, we join the global nonviolent movement for justice, disarmament and peace, because, in the end, all the world's struggles are connected. They form one struggle for nonviolence.

There are a billion ways to work for justice, disarmament and peace. We can join local projects against U.S. warmaking; nuclear weapons; catastrophic climate change; extreme poverty; the death penalty; hand gun violence; drone warfare; homelessness; hunger; racism; violence against women; or other forms of violence. We can try to stand in solidarity with the world's poor and with creation; side with the children of the world, the victims of our wars, those targeted by our militarism, creatures and creation itself. As we reach across national boundaries, we extend the

122

global outreach of loving nonviolence and subvert the imperial culture of war, killing and destruction.

We need them all. If everyone pitches in and does what he or she can, the grassroots movement will grow and become contagious and wear down even the most entrenched structures of violence and empire. That's how change happens. That's the way the God of peace works among us. *That* is the will of God. Through our public action, our campaigns, and our movements, the God of peace make the victory of nonviolence inevitable.

My friend Howard Zinn (the historian who wrote *A People's History of the United States)* told me with great emotion not long before he died that after a lifetime of studying all the social change movements in our history—the Abolitionists, the Suffragists, the Labor movement, the Civil Rights movement, the anti-Vietnam war movement—he realized that they all shared one common ingredient: every one in each of these movements was hopeless. They had no hope that they would live to see the change they worked for. But then he realized that they shared something else: every one refused to give up! Even though they knew they would not live to see the change they wanted, they kept working publicly for justice and peace. They never stopped. They knew it was the right thing to do, that this was the best work they could do with their lives. And so, every day these grassroots activists did one or two or three tasks for the movement. They did what they could and they kept at it. It was that persistent determination by millions of ordinary grassroots activists, Howard Zinn concluded, that made all the difference in our history.

Such determined movement building works. It wears down every obstacle, every intransigent system, every unjust social custom. If we can just get over the pessimistic, but apparently reasonable opinion that there's nothing that can be done, and go forward in good faith, doing what we can to help the movement, the change will occur. It's inevitable.

That, Howard Zinn told me, is the great lesson of our history. Keep at it, even if there is no hope on the horizon, even if we may not live to see the impossible change we seek. Don't give up. Keep organizing, speaking out and taking a stand. Together, we will make a difference.

If we keep at the struggle, we will discover new meaning and purpose in our lives. We will see how as ordinary members of a grassroots movement, we can actually make a difference in the world, and help relieve unjust human suffering and bring about new openings for justice and peace.

Even more, we will actively join the ongoing holy work of the God of peace to bring peace on earth. As we join Jesus' campaign of nonviolence and live out his Sermon on the Mount, we become mature Christian disciples. We carry on his mission to disarm and heal the world and herald the coming of God's peace. For that, we will receive his Beatitude blessing.

Nonviolence, historically, always works. It's the power of God acting through us for God's reign. All we have to do is get with program and pitch in. God will take care of the rest.

15

Movement Building, Protest Organizing, Truth-Telling, and Risk-Taking: The Work of the Nonviolent Activist

In 2005, fifteen-year-old Brazilian Mayara Vivian called on the people of Sao Paulo to protest their unjust poverty. A hundred people turned out to march and she was thrilled. She felt she was making an impact, so she kept at it. Once she started organizing, speaking out, and bringing people together for protests, she never stopped.

In June 2013, when she called for people to take to the streets to protest Brazil's proposed bus fare increase, she hoped for several hundred protesters. Fifty thousand turned out! She never imagined such that response. Within days, over 1.2 million people marched across Brazil demanding an end to poverty, unjust prices, and government corruption. "We never would have thought that one hundred thousand people would show up," she told *The New York Times* ("Sweeping Protests in Brazil Pull In An Array of Grievances," June 20, 2013). "It's like the taking of the Bastille."

Within days, Vivian's work led to protests in over 100 cities, threatening the government itself. "Much like the Occupy movement in the United States, the anticorruption protests that shook India in recent years, the demonstrations over living standards in Israel or the fury in European nations like Greece, the demonstrators in Brazil are fed up with traditional political structures, challenging the governing party and the opposition alike," *The Times* continued.

Like Mayara Vivian, nonviolent activists all over the world are discovering that if they call upon people to protest structured injustice and organize demonstrations, and most of all, keep at it, eventually people will respond. Movements begin to emerge organically. Change starts to unfold.

Today, people around the world are organizing as never before, building movements, speaking the truth, taking enormous personal risks, and working to topple systemic injustice and end war. Julian Assange, Bradley Manning and Edward Snowden, like Daniel Ellsberg in the 1970s, have given their lives for the truth, exposing the imperial law-breaking of the U.S. government. Their actions have inspired much organizing and movement-building.

Others have taken great risks, too, for justice and peace. A few years ago, a young man named Tim DeChristopher disrupted an illegal Bush Administration auction of U.S. park land in Utah to the oil companies, and saved tens of thousands of acres of pristine desert from oil drilling. Sister Megan Rice, Greg Bortje-Obed, and Michael Walli face decades in prison for peacefully protesting against U.S. nuclear weapons by walking onto the Oak Ridge Nuclear Production facility outside Knoxville, Tennessee. Medea Benjamin, cofounder of Code Pink, disrupted President Obama's speech on National Defense by shouting out questions about Guantanamo prisoners and the U.S. drone bombing program, among many other nonviolent actions. Through her group, Voices for Creative Nonviolence, Kathy Kelly has led dozens of delegations to Iraq and Afghanistan, and provides support to a dedicated group of young people committed to nonviolence in Kabul.

Since 9/11, thousands of nonviolent people have been arrested across the United States for protesting the U.S. wars in Iraq, Afghanistan, Libya, Pakistan and Yemen, the U.S. drone program, the proposed Keystone XL pipeline, the U.S. prison camp at Guantanamo, unjust U.S. immigration policies, and government corruption. The Occupy movement brought hundreds of thousands of people out on to the streets of America to protest corporate greed and government catering to the elite one percent at the expense of ninety nine percent of the rest of the population.

Much of this nonviolent resistance has been ignored or trivialized by the mainstream media, but as with every movement, change moves from the bottom up. Power never voluntarily relinquishes its control over populations, nations or the world. It has to be confronted, challenged, and resisted until the movement overflows onto the streets; alerts, educates, wins over and mobilizes the populace; becomes a reality the media cannot ignore; begins to change mainstream culture; and makes the change that once seemed impossible reasonable and then inevitable.

"It is from numberless diverse acts of courage and belief that human history is shaped," Robert F. Kennedy said in a 1966 speech in South Africa. "Each time a person stands up for an ideal, or acts to improve the lot of others, or strikes out against injustice, he or she sends forth a tiny ripple of hope, and crossing each other from a million different centers of energy and daring, those ripples build a current that can sweep down the mightiest walls of oppression and resistance."

No one told me these things when I was young. As I studied Gandhi, Dr. King, Dorothy Day, Daniel and Philip Berrigan, Cesar Chavez, Desmond Tutu, and other peace and justice leaders, I realized I had to get personally involved in the global movements for justice and peace. At the time, I couldn't find any local peace and justice group, so I started one. Within a short time, I was organizing demonstrations, protests, press conferences, prayer services for peace, public witnesses, civil disobedience actions and national mobilizations. Later, people asked me how to build movements and organize protests. Most of it comes down to hard work, common sense, systematic outreach, fundraising, and collaboration with as many good people as possible.

Martin Luther King, Jr.'s daughter Yolanda once said that if people really knew what happened in the Civil Rights movement, they would ask, "What can I do to help *today* in the struggle for justice and peace?" In the Civil Rights movement, everybody pitched in and the movement spread far and wide. Today, we too can each ask, "How can I help?" I think we all need to become activists, organizers, even local leaders. Each one of us has to pitch in with the nitty-gritty work of organizing protests, advertizing events, reaching out to our local community, educating the public, and building the grassroots movement. As we do, we find ourselves newly empowered and able to empower others to work for change.

"You may never know what results come from your action," Gandhi wrote, "but if you do nothing, there will be no result."

This is the life work of the nonviolent activist. It requires dedication, patience, faith, persistence and hope. In the face of war, poverty, nuclear weapons and catastrophic climate change, it is necessary work. More of us need to step up to the plate and do what we can. As we do, we can take heart knowing that we are in solidarity with millions of other activists around the world. Together we make a difference.

16

A Spirituality of Nonviolence for Gospel Movement People

"My optimism rests on my belief in the infinite possibilities of the individual to develop nonviolence," Gandhi once said. "The more you develop it in your own being, the more infectious it becomes until it overwhelms your surroundings and by and by might oversweep the world."

Like Gandhi, we are trying to develop the infinite possibilities of nonviolence in our own lives—in our very being—so that our creative nonviolence becomes contagious and touches everyone around us, and so that then, together we might help disarm the world. Like Gandhi, we explore nonviolence within ourselves and our relationships with all people, all creatures and creation, and through steadfast organized movements for social change. Gandhi invites us to experiment with the truth of nonviolence within ourselves, among our circle of people and publicly in the world of violence so that the Spirit and wisdom of nonviolence will spread, disarm, and bring peace.

As we practice an active nonviolence that reaches out to include the whole human race, we will quickly discover that we need something greater than the American dream to sustain us. We need the support of good friends, a local peace and justice group, the wider nonviolence movement, the lessons of the saints and peacemakers, our best spiritual wisdom, the beauty of creation itself—and the God of peace. In other words, we need a spirituality of active nonviolence, one that can sustain us for the lifelong struggle for disarmament, justice and peace that lies ahead of us.

As we ponder the three dimensions of nonviolence—toward ourselves, toward all people and creation, and our participation in the global grassroots movement—we can explore the spiritual side of this life journey. Here are some key ingredients for a spirituality of active nonviolence.

Trust the God of Peace

First of all, we place all our trust in the God of peace. That means, we no longer place any trust in guns, weapons, war, armies, drones, air force fighters, Trident submarines, militarism, or any instrument of violence. We know now that they not only do not end violence, they violate the will of the God of peace. We are done with violence and the idols of violence.

As we transfer our trust from weapons of war to the God of peace, we let go of our fear, anger and violence. We trust that the Creator, the God of nonviolence, knows what She is doing and will take care of us and the whole human race. Through our daily meditation, we cultivate this trust, dwell in God's presence, befriend God, let God love us and leave everything in God's hands. We know that everything belongs to God, including each one of us. Over time, through our daily meditation, we feel comfortable in God's loving protection, and so we do not worry or get anxious. We even lose our fear of death. Indeed, this growing trust makes us peaceful and ready to face anything—sickness or health, prosperity or misfortune, joy or pain, life or death. We go forward in a spirit of peace rooted in our conscious relationship with the God of peace.

We take heart knowing that our God is nonviolent, loving and compassionate. We become our true selves through our relationship with this loving God, and seek to fulfill our identities as God's beloved sons and daughters. As we center ourselves in God and God's peace, and grow in trust, we deepen our nonviolence. We center ourselves in God's peace. Each step of this journey of faith, hope and trust in the God of peace leads us to the next step. We may only get enough light for just the next step—not the rest of our life's journey—which is why trust in the God of peace becomes so central to our peacemaking lives.

Open Your Heart in Universal Love

As we trust in God, we also widen our hearts in universal love for all human beings. We recognize everyone as our very sister and brother. We seek, cultivate and practice universal nonviolent love, with compassion toward all sentient beings, regardless of any difference, such as race, gender, age, class, ability, nationality, and religion. We love those around us and carry out that attitude of universal love toward humanity and creation as best we can. We celebrate human diversity and welcome new people with interest, curiosity, and concern, knowing that they are our sisters and brothers. Through our prayer and meditation, we know that one day in eternity we will dwell in peace and wholeness with every human being who ever lived, so we seek to live out that vision now by befriending everyone we meet.

As we love those we meet and remain open to loving every living human being, we also seek to serve and help everyone, especially those in most need. Attending to those in most need—the poor, hungry, wounded, sick, imprisoned, marginalized and disenfranchised—marks our inner attitude of universal love. We try to care for those not being cared for. We do for others what we wish they would do for us. This heart of universal love, which is central to every major religion, becomes the new normal: a spiritual way of life for us. Over time, it gets hard-wired into our neuron pathways, so that our spirit, our bodies, and our minds lead us to love everyone.

Conscious Mindfulness

As we reach out in universal love, we also practice a steady mindfulness to stay centered and conscious in a spirit of peace and calmness. Between the hectic day-to-day life of the fast lane, the global crises that cry out for our attention, problems in our personal lives, family, work and church life, we easily lose our center. Indeed, violence is the natural fruit of "mindlessness"—not being aware or conscious of the present moment, living in the unconscious chaos of war.

Nonviolence invites us to a daily, moment by moment mindfulness, where we are aware of the present moment, even our breath and our feelings. We attempt to stay centered in that present moment of peace, aware of negative or hard feelings as they come and go, aware of exciting or happy feelings as these too come and go, aware of all the thoughts and concerns that pass through our minds. The life of peace leads us inevitably into the present moment of peace and the practice of staying in that moment so that we are not tossed one way or another, but centered like a mountain in the here and now of peace.

Buddhist master Thich Nhat Hanh has spent his life teaching the ancient wisdom of mindfulness as an antidote to the culture of violence. Mindlessness is antithetical to the nonviolent life, but it has become the norm. We are like ghosts, or zombies. When we are "mindless," we are not in our true selves. Instead we are stuck in the past or the future and unable to wake up to the present. Nhat Hanh recommends mindful walking, mindful eating, and mindful meditation as ordinary helpful practices that can strengthen us to return to our breathing and the present moment, and keep us on the even keel of peace.

"We need a collective awakening," he writes. "Most people are still sleeping. Mindfulness is at the heart of awakening, of enlightenment. We practice breathing to be able to be here in the present moment so that we can recognize what is happening in us and around us. We all have a great desire to be able to live in peace and to have environmental sustainability. What most of us don't yet have are concrete ways of making our commitment to sustainable living a reality in our daily lives. It's time for each of us to wake up and take action in our own lives. If we awaken to our true situation, there will be a change in our collective consciousness."(in *Spiritual Ecology*, Llewellyn Vaughan-Lee, ed. Golden Sufi Center, 2013, 26-28).

Mindfulness is a key ingredient in the spirituality of nonviolence and peace.

Long Haul Vision

Spiritually-alive nonviolence upholds the vision of a whole new world of peace.

Violence is the fruit of our collective blindness. We are the blind leading the blind, and we're going over the cliff to our own destruction, and we don't even know it. Our lack of vision, our global blindness, has led us to this catastrophic moment with nuclear weapons, unparalleled corporate greed, widespread apathy in the face of starvation, and environmental destruction.

Nonviolence calls us to recognize the blindness that leads to our global violence, to renounce our systemic violence, and to put on the glasses of peace so that we will be able to see the way forward into a new world of peace.

Nonviolence prompts us to reclaim our imagination for peace by envisioning a new world of peace. One of the first casualties of war is the loss of the imagination; people cannot imagine peace. Nowadays few can imagine a world without war, poverty or nuclear weapons. People of nonviolence, on the other hand, use their imaginations and help others see what peace looks like.

This is what Jesus did. He was a great visionary of peace and universal love who pointed people toward the reign of God— God's realm of peace, love and nonviolence, which he said was *at hand*. The reign of God must be our goal, he taught—not empire, money, status or security. He inspired people to welcome God's reign of peace among us and within us.

As people of visionary nonviolence, we, too, can point people toward the reign of God by saying, "The time has come to create a new world without war, violence, injustice, starvation, killing, nuclear weapons, or environmental destruction." As we help people re-imagine reality and the coming of a new world of nonviolence, we inspire them to join our campaign and to mobilize others to make this vision of peace come true.

Nonviolence takes a long haul view of reality—historical, biblical, spiritual. It sees the God of peace offering us a new world of peace. It knows that humanity is capable of making dramatic shifts for the better by remembering how it abolished cannibalism and slavery. It inspires us similarly to abolish war, poverty, nuclear weapons, and environmental destruction. Most of all, visionary nonviolence helps people see their way out of the darkness of violence and into the new light of peace. By establishing the boundaries of nonviolence, it sets new guidelines to resolve every conflict nonviolently. Through the lens of nonviolence, we can see a new way to live and the coming of a better world.

The Cross and Resurrection

People of Gospel nonviolence fundamentally are people who participate in the Paschal Mystery—the death and resurrection of Jesus—as the way toward social, economic and political change. As followers of Jesus, we walk the way of the cross in nonviolent resistance to structural injustice, war, and empire. Like the nonviolent Jesus, we enter the struggle, speak out, take risks, engage in nonviolent direct action, and accept the consequences of our public stand—harassment, persecution, estrangement, arrest, trial, imprisonment and maybe even death. We even learn with Dr. King to use voluntary suffering creatively as a tool in the nonviolent struggle for justice and peace. Instead of killing others, we are willing to undergo being killed in the struggle for justice and peace; instead of inflicting violence on others, we accept suffering without even the desire to retaliate with further violence as we pursue justice with love for all people. We try to unite our

134

suffering for justice and peace with Jesus' suffering and death, and the crucified peoples of the world. As we give our lives in nonviolent love, like Jesus, for the human race, our suffering is transformed and we participate in God's disarming, redemptive work. The fall of empire is assured.

But we are not only people of the cross. People of Gospel nonviolence are also people of resurrection. As we walk the way of the cross in nonviolent resistance to the culture of war and injustice, we are practicing resurrection, getting ready for resurrection. As we look to the risen Christ, we take heart, renew our hope, and know that death does not get the last word.

With the risen Jesus, there is real reason for hope. His way of nonviolence has proven true. God has granted ultimate approval over his mission to disarm and heal humanity through creative, loving nonviolence, and therefore, called humanity to join that mission as people of Gospel nonviolence. As we try to engage in creative nonviolence and work for justice, disarmament and peace, we know that God blesses our work, sides with this work, and joins the effort to transform the world nonviolently. Our nonviolent lives fit within the framework of Jesus' nonviolent life and mission, and so they take on a new eschatological purpose. As we discover God in this work for peace, we deepen our spiritual roots and find new strength, grace and hope to spend our lives in the struggle for justice and disarmament.

When the nonviolent Jesus rose from the dead, he said to his friends over and over again, "Peace be with you." He showed no trace of violence, vengeance, retaliation, anger or resentment. Instead, he comforted his friends, made breakfast for them, and invited them once again to follow him. He was as nonviolent as ever, even more so, if that were possible.

People of resurrection welcome the risen Christ's resurrection gift of peace. We slowly realize the depth of his divine nonviolence, so we accept his greeting of peace, take it to heart, place our hope in his risen presence, and go forward in his footsteps on the way of nonviolence, doing what we can, leaving the outcome to God.

As resurrection people, we know that our survival is already guaranteed, that God will take care of us. As we carry on Jesus' work of peace and give our lives in nonviolent resistance to injustice and war, we remain confident that we too will share in his resurrection and live on in his realm of eternal peace and love. This is good news. It means we have plenty of reason for hope, and new energy to carry on with the great work to be done.

The historic student-led demonstrations in France in 1968 rung with a chant that is as apt today as it was then: "Be reasonable. Demand the impossible."

Like those French protesters, practitioners of nonviolence are reasonable people who demand the impossible. With our spirituality of nonviolence and peace we trust in the God of peace, open our hearts in universal love, maintain a conscious mindfulness, see with a long haul vision, and willingly risk the cross and the resurrection as the way to nonviolent social change. We root our life journey of nonviolence in the God of peace, the nonviolent Jesus, and the Holy Spirit of peace and love so that we become one with the universe, with heaven and earth, and all the saints and martyrs and peacemakers who have gone before us on the path of peace.

This spiritual framework, context and practice gives each one of us the strength to live a nonviolent life. We have enough strength to step out into the world as people of peace, love and nonviolence, rooted and grounded in a whole new spirituality, fashioned on Jesus himself.

Questions for Personal Reflection
and Small Group Discussion

When have you seen the power of active nonviolence work, in your own life and in the public movements for justice and peace? What conclusions do you draw from the new book, *Why Civil Resistance Works*, which argues that nonviolent movements achieve far better ends than violent movements? What does that mean for us as we face the global crises of today?

Do you agree with Dr. King's principles of nonviolence and steps for action in a nonviolent movement? How are you already living according to these principles and putting these steps into action? Which ones challenge you the most? How can you live more and more according to his principles and put those steps into action to help build up the global grassroots movement of nonviolence?

What touches you, inspires you, and challenges you about the 1963 Birmingham and the Birmingham Pledge of nonviolence? What other campaigns and movements inspire you to carry on the work of movement building, protest organizing, truth-telling and risk-taking for justice and peace?

What nonviolent movements and nonviolent actions have you participated in? Where do we see the hope and power of active nonviolence working in the world today? What new nonviolent public action can you undertake for justice and peace? What global grassroots movement of nonviolence are you part of or do you wish to join?

How can we help fulfill Gandhi's dream, "to make truth and nonviolence not matters for mere individual practice but for practice by groups and communities and nations"?

What ingredients would you include in a spirituality of nonviolence and peace? How do you trust in God; open yourself in universal love; practice conscious mindfulness; maintain a long haul vision of peace; and participate in the cross and resurrection of the nonviolent Jesus?

What sustains you for the long haul work of peacemaking? What gives you hope? Where do you find the God of peace in your life of active nonviolence?

How can you integrate the three dimensions of nonviolence more fully into your life—practicing nonviolence toward yourself and all others as well as joining the global grassroots movement of nonviolence?

Conclusion

Active nonviolence offers you and me a way out of the world's mad violence and a way forward into the light and life of God's peace. It invites us to reject violence once and for all. It suggests that we no longer need to nurture violence within us, or manifest violence toward others, or treat animals and the earth violently, or remain powerless in the face of the world's systemic injustice, warmaking, nuclear weapons and destructive policies. We have a power at our disposal, a weapon of love and truth, that we are still just learning.

With nonviolence, as Gandhi and King insisted, the days of violence are coming to an end. With every choice and action for nonviolence, we begin a new era in human history. This new age will be rooted in the best of spirituality, theology, and morality, the best in all of us for all of us. As we deepen nonviolence in every aspect of life, we herald the coming of a nonviolent world, a world without war, hunger, killings, executions, nuclear weapons, or environmental destruction. There can be no better use of our lives. Along the way, we fulfill our calling to become sons and daughters of the God of peace. We directly serve the coming of God's reign of peace on earth.

The nonviolent life, as we have emphasized in these pages, involves three dimensions: practicing nonviolence toward ourselves, so that we cultivate inner peace and claim our union with the God of peace; practicing nonviolence toward all others, all creatures and all creation, so that love and justice can spread far and wide, and creation itself is protected; and practicing nonviolence by joining the global grassroots movement of nonviolence, so that more and more of us participate in the struggles to end war, poverty, nuclear weapons, environmental destruction and all forms of structural violence, and make inevitable greater breakthroughs for justice and disarmament.

As we understand the nonviolence of Gandhi and King more and more, we realize the necessity of practicing all three dimensions simultaneously. We determine not to repeat the mistakes of our movement ancestors, but to stand on their shoulders and go farther down the road toward peace. As we do, we can become, like Gandhi and King, transforming people of active nonviolence—saints, prophets, apostles, teachers, healers, and champions of God's peace.

We can do this. We can live a nonviolent life. We can welcome God's gift of peace within us, among us, and in the world. We have more power than we realize. Each one of us has the power of the God of peace within us, if we dare believe and act on that faith. We can make peace our home, and help turn the earth into a home of peace for everyone.

And so I end our reflection the way I began, with a prayer to the God of peace asking for help to become peacemakers, people who live the nonviolent life to the full:

God of peace, thank you for inviting me to the life of nonviolence, to become a peacemaker, your beloved son/daughter.

Give me the grace to be nonviolent to myself, that I may make peace with myself, welcome your spirit of peace within me, and radiate personally your peaceful presence.

Give me the grace to be nonviolent to all others, all creatures, and all creation, that I may love everyone as my sister and brother, and help protect humanity, your creatures and creation that your reign of peace may be a living reality.

And give me the grace to serve your global grassroots movement of nonviolence, that I may do my part to help end war, poverty, racism, sexism, nuclear weapons, systemic injustice and environmental destruction, that more and more people will welcome your wisdom of nonviolence and work diligently for disarmament and justice that your peace may one day be realized everywhere on earth.

Thank you, God of peace, for all the blessings of peace, hope, life and love that you give me. Make me an instrument of your peace, and I will offer you the gift of a nonviolent life well lived, for your greater glory. Amen.

Acknowledgments

I thank my friends and co-workers at Pace e Bene for their help and support with this project and for all they do to promote nonviolence: Fr. Louie Vitale, O.F.M., L.R. Berger, Veronica Pelicaric, Jerica Arents, Kit Evans, Ryan Hall and Ken Butigan. You are the best peace group in the country!

Thanks to Carmelita Laura Valdes Damron for the use of her beautiful artwork for the cover. I'm so grateful!

A big shout out to my friends who've accompanied me through this project and my own struggles with the nonviolent life: Danny O'Regan, Barbara and Jim Reale, Renea Roberts and Mat Crimmins, Janet and Martin Sheen, Nancy and John Cusack, Arch., Sr. Helen Prejean, Sr. Margaret Maggio, Danny Muller, Joe Cosgrove, Harry Geib, S.J., Bill Sneck, S.J., Steve Kelly, S.J., Daniel Berrigan, S.J., George Anderson, S.J., Chris Boles, S.J., Eric DeBode, Maria Decsy, Mairead Maguire, Kathy Kelly, Anna and David Smith, Roshi Joan Halifax, Ed DeBerri, Ellie Voutselas, Bud Ryan, Ray East, Patti Normile, Shelley and Jim Douglass, Natalie Goldberg, Mark and Richard Deats, Pat O'Brien, Jack Marth, Ben Jimenez, Jim Fickey, Patrick Hart, Carole Powell, Joe Schmidt and the Afghan Peace Volunteers.

Special thanks to Ryan Hall of Pace e Bene for his great generosity working with me to bring this book to life—despite my endless emails, calls, questions, suggestions, and publishing issues. Pace e Bene to you, Ryan!

Most of all, I thank Pace e Bene director, Ken Butigan, my friend and co-worker, who's been an inspiration to me for decades, and is one of the unsung heroes of the peace movement. Thank you, Ken, for inviting me to join the Pace e Bene team. Thank you for all your help over the years encouraging my own journey of nonviolence. Thank you for your gracious foreword. And thank you for all your hard work on this manuscript. You've not only made a better book, you've enriched my life with your kindness, generosity and friendship. You, Ken, show me what the nonviolent life looks like. Thank you. Pace e Bene always!

I offer this little book as a gift to my friends Dar and Patty, two of the best "recruiters for the Universe" that I know. May we always sing the songs of peace and love!

And may the God of peace bless us all!

Suggested Readings

Ackerman, Peter and Duvall, Jack. *A Force More Powerful: A Century of Nonviolent Conflict* (New York: St. Martin's Press, 2000).

Berrigan, Daniel. *To Dwell in Peace* (Oregon: Wipf and Stock, 2007 edition).

Brockman, James. *Romero: A Life* (Maryknoll: Orbis, 2005).

Butigan, Ken (with Bruno, Patricia). *From Violence to Wholeness: The Spirituality and Practice of Active Nonviolence* (Pace e Bene Press, 2002).

—(with Pelicaric, Veronica; Preston-Pile, Ken; and Slattery, Laura). *Engage: Exploring Nonviolent Living* (Pace e Bene Press, 2005).

—(with Litell, Mary, and Vitale, Louis). *Franciscan Nonviolence* (Pace e Bene Press, 2003).

Chernus, Ira. *American Nonviolence.* (Maryknoll: Orbis, 2004).

Chenoweth, Erica and Stephan, Maria. *Why Civil Resistance Works: The Strategic Logic of Nonviolent Conflict* (New York: Columbia Univ. Press, 2012).

Day, Dorothy. *The Duty of Delight: Diaries* (Edited by Robert Ellsberg) (Milwaukee: Marquette Univ. Press, 2008).

Dear, John. *A Persistent Peace* (Chicago: Loyola Press, 2008).

—*Daniel Berrigan: Essential Writings* (Ed.) (Maryknoll: Orbis Books, 2011).

—*Jesus the Rebel* (Sheed and Ward/Rowman and Littlefield, 2000).

—*Living Peace* (New York: Doubleday, 2000).

—*Mohandas Gandhi: Essential Writings* (Ed.) (Maryknoll: Orbis Books, 2002).

—*The God of Peace: Toward a Theology of Nonviolence* (Oregon: Wipf and Stock, 2008).

Douglass, James. *Lightning East to West* (Oregon: Wipf and Stock, 2006).

—*Resistance and Contemplation* (Oregon: Wipf and Stock, 2006).

—*The Nonviolent Coming of God* (Oregon: Wipf and Stock, 2006).

—*The Nonviolent Cross* (Oregon: Wipf and Stock, 2006).

Easwaran, Eknath. *Gandhi the Man.* (Berkeley: Nilgiri Press, 1997).

Ediger, Peter (Ed.) *Living with the Wolf: Walking the Way of Nonviolence* (Pace e Bene Press, 2009).

Ellison, Sharon. *Taking the War Out of Our Words: The Powerful Art of Non-Defensive Communication* (www.pndc.com).

Fahey, Joseph and Armstrong, Richard (Ed.) *A Peace Reader* (New York: Paulist Press, 1992).

Fischer, Louis. *The Life of Mahatma Gandhi* (New York: Harper & Row, 1954).

Forest, Jim. *All Is Grace: A Biography of Dorothy Day* (Maryknoll: Orbis, 2011).

—*Living With Wisdom: A Life of Thomas Merton* (Maryknoll: Orbis, 2008).

Hanh, Thich Nhat. *Being Peace* (Berkeley: Parallex Press, 1987).

—*Creating True Peace* (New York: Free Press, 2003).

144

—*Peace Is Every Breath* (New York: HarperOne, 2011).

—*Peace Is Every Step* (New York: Bantam, 1991).

Holmes, Richard (Ed.) *Nonviolence In Theory and Practice* (Calif: Wadsworth Pub., 1990).

King, Martin L. Jr. *Stride Toward Freedom* (New York: Harper & Row, 1958).

King, Mary. *Mahatma Gandhi and Martin Luther King, Jr.: The Power of Nonviolent Action* (France: UNESCO Pub., 1999).

Long, Michael (Ed.) *Christian Peace and Nonviolence: A Documentary History* (Maryknoll: Orbis, 2011).

Lynd, Staughton, and Lynd, Alice (Eds.) *Nonviolence in America* (Maryknoll: Orbis, 1995).

Merton, Thomas. *Passion for Peace: The Social Essays.* (Edited by William Shannon) (New York: Crossroad, 1995).

Nagler, Michael. *The Search for a Nonviolent Future* (San Francisco: Inner Ocean, 2004).

Nouwen, Henri. *Peacework* (Maryknoll: Orbis, 2005).

—*The Road to Peace* (Ed. by John Dear) (Maryknoll: Orbis, 1997).

Powers, Roger and Vogele, William (Eds.) *Protest, Power and Change: An Encyclopedia of Nonviolent Action* (New York: Garland Pub., 1997).

Putz, Erna (Ed.) *Franz Jagerstatter: Letters and Writings from Prison* (Maryknoll: Orbis, 2009).

Rosenberg, Marshall. *Nonviolent Communication* (Calif.: Puddle Dancer Press, 2003).

Sharp, Gene. *The Politics of Nonviolent Action* (three volumes) (Boston: Porter Sargent, 1973).

—*Waging Nonviolent Struggle: 20ᵗʰ Century Practice and 21ˢᵗ Century Potential* (Boston: Porter Sargent, 2005).

The Power of Nonviolence: A Beacon Anthology (Boston: Beacon Press, 2002).

Vanderhaar, Gerard. *Active Nonviolence* (Wipf and Stock, 2013).

—*Personal Nonviolence* (Pax Christi USA, 2006).

Washington, James M. *A Testament of Hope: The Essential Writings of Martin Luther King, Jr.* (San Francisco: Harper and Row, 1986).

Watley, William. *Roots of Resistance: The Nonviolent Ethic of Martin Luther King Jr.* (Valley Forge: Judson Press, 1985).

Wink, Walter. *Engaging the Powers* (Minneapolis: Fortress Press, 1992).

—*Jesus and Nonviolence: A Third Way* (Minneapolis: Fortress Press, 2003).

—*Peace Is the Way: Writings on Nonviolence from the Fellowship of Reconciliation* (Ed.) (Maryknoll: Orbis, 2000).

Yoder, John Howard. *The Politics of Jesus* (Grand Rapids, Mich.: Eerdmans Pub., 1994).

About Pace e Bene

Pace e Bene Nonviolence Service fosters peace, justice and the well-being of all through education, community-building and action for nonviolent change. It has facilitated 700 nonviolence workshops for 30,000 people in the United States and around the world; organized or participated in numerous movements for nonviolent change; and through Pace e Bene Press has published numerous books and manuals.

Pace e Bene (pronounced *pah-chay bay nay*) means "peace and all good" in Italian. St. Francis of Assisi used this expression as a greeting and as a means of proclaiming the way of peace in the midst of a violent world.

Founded in 1989, Pace e Bene Nonviolence Service offers resources to assist in the journey of personal and social transformation, such as retreats, workshops, presentations, classes, and a variety of publications. For Pace e Bene, nonviolence is more than a principle for effective protest—it is a way of life. For over two decades, Pace e Bene's unique approach has been transforming lives and reaching people around the globe by tapping into participants fearlessness and empathy—and unleashing the power of nonviolent change.

Pace e Bene's staff and associates engage in nonviolent action and work together with countless individuals, organizations, and movements to strengthen their efforts to end war, protect human rights, challenge injustice, and to meet today's profound spiritual task: to build a more just and peaceful world.

Pace e Bene has staff and associates in Chicago, Illinois; Los Angeles, California; Oakland, California; Santa Fe, New Mexico; Concord, New Hampshire; Montreal, Quebec, Canada; Perth, Australia; Plateau State, Nigeria; and a growing network of collaborators in North and South America. We are available to lead one-day and weekend workshops in local communities utilizing the resources and tools from our acclaimed book, *Engage: Exploring Nonviolent Living*.

In 2013 Pace e Bene launched *Campaign Nonviolence*, a national movement to transform our lives and to change our world through the power of active nonviolence. Campaign Nonviolence seeks to put into practice the three crucial components in John Dear's book *The Nonviolent Life*—practicing nonviolence toward ourselves; practicing nonviolence toward all others, all creatures and all creation; and practicing nonviolence by joining the global movement to abolish war, end poverty, stop the destruction of the earth and foster a just and peaceful world for all.

Please visit our website **www.paceebene.org**; order more books and resources; invite us to lead workshops on nonviolence; and join this great mission to help build a global grassroots movement of nonviolence!

About the Author

"John Dear is the embodiment of a peacemaker," Archbishop Desmond Tutu wrote a few years ago when he nominated John for the Nobel Peace Prize. "He has led by example through his actions and in his writings and in numerous sermons, speeches and demonstrations. He believes that peace is not something static, but rather to make peace is to be engaged, mind, body and spirit. His teaching is to love yourself, to love your neighbor, your enemy, and to love the world and to understand the profound responsibility in doing all of these. He is a man who has the courage of his convictions and who speaks out and acts against war, the manufacture of weapons and any situation where a human being might be at risk through violence. For evil to prevail requires only that good people sit on the sidelines and do nothing. John Dear is compelling all of us to stand up and take responsibility for the suffering of humanity so often caused through selfishness and greed."

John Dear has spent over three decades speaking to people around the world about the Gospel of Jesus, the way of nonviolence and the call to make peace. He has served as the director of the Fellowship of Reconciliation, the largest interfaith peace organization in the United States, and after September 11, 2001, as one of the Red Cross coordinators of chaplains at the Family Assistance Center, and counseled thousands of relatives and rescue workers. He has worked in homeless shelters, soup kitchens, and community centers; traveled in warzones around the world, including Iraq, Palestine, Nicaragua, Afghanistan, and Colombia; lived in El Salvador, Guatemala and Northern Ireland; been arrested over 75 times in acts of civil disobedience against war; and spent eight months in prison for a Plowshares disarmament action. In the 1990s, he arranged for Mother Teresa to speak to various governors to stop the death penalty. He has two Master's Degrees in Theology from the Graduate Theological

Union in California, and has taught theology at Fordham University.

John Dear has been featured in *The New York Times, The Washington Post, USA Today, National Public Radio's "All Things Considered"* and elsewhere. He writes a weekly blog for the *National Catholic Reporter* (at www.ncronline.org) and is featured regularly on the national radio show, "Democracy Now!" and the Huffington Post. He is the subject of the DVD documentary, "The Narrow Path" (with music by Joan Baez and Jackson Browne). He is profiled in *John Dear On Peace*, by Patti Normile (St. Anthony Messenger Press, 2009). His nearly thirty books have been translated into ten languages. John Dear is on the staff of Pace e Bene.

For further information, see: www.johndear.org.

25722484R00094

Made in the USA
Charleston, SC
12 January 2014